PLEASE
STOP
PRAYING

By **Sally Edwards Danley**

Please Stop Praying

Please Stop Praying

Copyright © 2014 Sally Edwards Danley

All rights reserved.

ISBN: 1494904748
ISBN-13:978-149490746

Introduction
Please Stop Praying...

In the 1970s, my church had teachings on doing healing prayer. I was awed to have been given that Spiritual gift. We prayed as the Bible tells us in Romans 12 and 1 Corinthians 12. All the gifts of the Spirit were practiced at my church at that time.

Years later I was at a meeting of business people. During a break time, a young man came from across the room. He smiled and asked, "Aren't you Sally Danley?"

Smiling back, I nodded.

Then he said, "**Please stop praying** for my wife and I to have a baby. Five years ago we came to you and your prayer team during healing time one Sunday evening. We hadn't been able to get pregnant. You and your team prayed for us to have a baby.

Since your team prayed over us, <u>we've had four boys</u>! **Please stop praying**."

His broad grin showed his love of the Lord and his gratitude.

Each story in this book is of UNUSUAL HEALINGS.

Dedication

Please Stop Praying is dedicated to my three adult children who are wonderful individuals and have delighted me with many grandchildren and even Great Grandchildren.

Humor has been a big factor in our home.

As teens they all became self-supporting in good lines of work; nursing, a commercial artist and a teacher. They each became self-sufficient when they were able to purchase their own cars.

They were raised in church and Sunday school, and have been praying since they were old enough to talk. Jesus Christ has His covering over all of my offspring.

None of us are perfect. We love each other anyway.

PHILIPPIANS 4:8

PLEASE STOP PRAYING
CONTENTS

Please Stop Praying

Chapter	Title	Page #
1.	Migraine is Healed	8
2.	A Hypocrite In a Bottle	17
3.	The Modern Day Jesus	26
4.	Truth Washes Away Pain	34
5.	Death Bed Forgiveness	41
6.	God Saves the Rebel	49
7.	Forgiveness in Heaven	59
8.	Closing Doors to the Past	67
9.	Unbeliever is Healed	75
10.	Healing Priority to Babies	83
11.	A Battle with Darkness	90
12.	Smiles Covering Pain	99

CONTENTS
Continued:

Chapter	Title	Page #
13.	Poison Ivy Healed	107
14.	A Surprise Song	114
15.	Good Touch, Bad Touch	121
16.	More Than a Face Lift	132
17.	A Fallen Tree Brings Healing	139
18.	Resting In The Spirit?	149
19.	Blind More Ways Than One	156
20.	Miracles of Brain Surgery	162

Acknowledgements

I would never have had the courage to put this book together if it were not for the people of the **Heart of America Christian Writers' Network (H.A.C.W.N.)** which is based in Metropolitan Kansas City.

Jeanette Gardner Littleton honored me by asking me to be one of the writers she called together 27 years ago to start this group. THANK YOU HACWN TEAM.

Chapter #1

Migraine is Healed

"The body is a unit, though it is made up of many parts; and though all its parts are many, they form one body." I Corinthians 12:12 NIV

"Sally, my name is Betty Sue. Linda, from church, gave me your number and said you might be able to do some healing prayer for me."

Through the telephone line, her rich Southern drawl warmed my heart. It brought memories of my own Southern up-bringing.

Betty Sue asked me to come to her home and pray for her migraine headaches. I heard her choking back tears when she told me of a 25-year battle with the pain.

I spoke of memory healing prayer and she asked me to explain it. I did, and she was eager to make an appointment for me to come to her home to pray.

When my prayer partner, Marcia, and I entered Betty Sue's fine old brownstone in mid-town Kansas City, I felt as if I had taken a step back in time.

The "Old World" charm suited this immaculately dressed lady. Even her neat hairdo was similar to styles of the '40s.

Her home enveloped her in a cozy cocoon of elegance with its rich woodwork and antiques. She displayed delicate china and crystal. Elaborate oriental rugs covered the polished hardwood floors in every room.

She handed us our tea in china cups with saucers. Then Marcia and I followed her upstairs to a cozy sitting room furnished with a brocaded settee and two matching chairs. Walnut end-tables each had small lace doilies. It was a most pleasant setting.

After a few minutes of polite chatting, I asked Betty Sue to explain her prayer need in more detail.

With her eyebrows scrunched in emotional pain, she said, "I have been married for 25 years but have recently separated from my husband. His physical roughness with me when he's drunk is just too much.

I can't take it anymore. I know God doesn't like divorce but I feel He has given me permission to protect myself. So I'm moving back to Shreveport to be with my family."

Her slight smile showed her eagerness to return to her childhood home.

Then she said, "Please keep this confidential. None of my friends at church know about my plan.

"Over the years I've probably spent at least $50,000 for doctors, medicine and hospital bills trying to get these horrid migraines to stop. But nothing helps. I can't stand them any longer. I'm feeling one coming on right now."

As tears came, she grabbed her head and shook it as if trying to shake away the pain. "Please, Sally, do something."

At my suggestion, she took a deep breath, relaxed and was able to continue.

"And I must tell you, I'm a little frightened about this memory healing prayer you tried to explain to me. "But I do trust God will heal me. And my friends spoke highly of your gentle ministering of prayers."

"Betty Sue, I assure you that feeling scared is normal," I said softly trying to help her feel safe. I explained that Marcia and I had heard many secrets like hers from praying for others. I also told her about how we'd been taught to erase the memories from our minds after we pray with someone. After all, she was trusting two strangers in a new situation.

In conclusion I assured her, "And a team of intercessors are praying for us, as they do every time Marcia and I go to pray. Actually I even told them your name was Mary, to protect your privacy."

That seemed to bring her some comfort.

After I asked a few more questions we agreed it was time to begin.

"Let's put aside our cups of tea, and sit back and relax," I suggested.

Carefully placing my cup on the table, I bowed my head and began praying.

"Lord Jesus, we invite you to come and guide us to the place in Betty Sue's past where you know healing is needed."

It seemed God wanted to take her back to a time when she was nearly a teen. I saw a scene like a Winslow Homer painting from the early 1900s. Brilliant sunshine shimmered across a field as a little girl of about twelve, in an ankle-length dress, ran through the tall golden grasses, her bonnet flying from the tie around her neck. Assuming it was Betty Sue at that age, I began to describe the inviting scene.

Suddenly she screamed "No! No! I don't want to be there. I don't want to remember that."

Shocked, I opened my eyes and I saw Betty Sue curled against the back of the settee, covering her face with both hands.

I was shaken by her unexpected response and thought I had really blown it. That reaction was totally opposite of what I had expected.

I glanced at Marcia. Our eye contact gave unspoken agreement to remain silent. Silently we prayed for intervention of the Holy Spirit. Our Lord was working and peace settled over us all quickly.

We waited.

Praying silently again, we asked the Holy Spirit to draw Betty Sue out and give her the courage to explain. That would show us what was needed next. I've found that God's guidance is usually more clear when we're silent and listening.

Finally, through tears, Betty Sue explained what old memory she had screamed about. "I was barely twelve the day my teen-aged cousin, Chester, took me out into a sunny field to play. We were running. Suddenly he over-powered me and raped me. I was confused and shaken and raced home in tears."

She explained how she had run into the kitchen and thrown her arms around her mother and, between sobs, told her what had happened.

But Betty Sue was stunned when her mother said, "That couldn't have happened. Chester would never do such a thing. Don't you ever speak of that again." She pushed the child away and continued her work.

Confused by her mother's angry denial, and in a state of shock, the child dutifully obeyed and went to her bedroom.

Over the next few months, Betty Sue eventually was able to cram that memory into a dark corner of her subconscious, hoping to forget it. She never spoke of it again.

With that clear information, I began to pray aloud. Speaking softly, I invited Jesus to join Betty Sue at that time in her history. I suggested she envision Him entering her room. As He entered, I spoke what I was seeing.

He sat down beside the confused child on the bed. Jesus embraced her like a loving father.

I shared His words out loud. "My child you have done nothing wrong. This was not your fault. Chester was confused by his new manly feelings. He was wrong to hurt you like that. I weep with you in your pain and distress and am sorry that you had to go through that terrible experience."

Betty Sue began to uncurl on the settee. We knew she was accepting the words of Jesus.

With the Lord speaking, eventually she was able to experience forgiveness of her family. It took some time, since her pain had been held in so long.

Finally, in her vision of Jesus holding her as they sat in her childhood bedroom, she wrapped her arms around his neck and said. "Thank you, Jesus, for taking away my confusion and hurt."

He smiled, kissed her on the cheek, and said, "Don't forget. I'm always here. Just call my name." Then he quietly arose and disappeared.

At that point, I spoke the words needed to lead Betty Sue back to the present time.

After that prayer time, I was confident Jesus would continue to bring healing of that memory.

When I said "Amen", Betty Sue opened her eyes. They sparkled with joy.

Her hands cupped her head and she said, "It's gone! My migraine is completely gone!"

As we spoke of that long-held secret, Betty Sue admitted that her mother's words that day were confusing and frightening. Keeping silent about the incident all these years, deep inside she was now aware of feelings of guilt and shame, and confusion.

Discussing it, she realized the migraines had begun the day after her marriage. Suddenly it was apparent that the physical act of consummating the marriage stirred the painful memory, causing that first migraine.

Tightly held secrets obviously cause damage to our bodies.

With the shameful secret healed, the migraines were no more. Her countenance was transformed from a strained-looking lady of elegance to a vivacious servant of Christ.

At church the next Sunday, grinning widely, she proclaimed, "I'm a walking miracle!"

Betty Sue continued to be joyous and wanted to join me in praying with another woman with migraines.

She was eager to spread the love of Jesus Christ by passing on the fact that God still heals.

Please Stop Praying

Chapter #2

A Hypocrit In A Bottle

"Wine is a mocker, strong drink is raging: and whosoever is deceived thereby is not wise."
Proverbs 20:1

"How many of you know what a shrike is?" No one in the audience responded to that minister's question. We sat in a quaint old church in Moberly, Missouri. Dozens of us there were puzzled about that term. What did that have to do with healing prayer?

Sharply dressed, with his neat mustache and strong voice, the visiting minister was well-known. He'd flown in from California to teach us how to administer healing prayer. I'd read his books and had great respect for his ministry and healing teachings.

He continued, "If you don't know, it's because some areas of the country refer to church hypocrites as shrikes. Are you a shrike?"

He seemed to be looking straight at me when he spit out that word "shrike".

Why did I want to totally slide down under the church pew? Guilt overwhelmed me.

Driving back home to Kansas City, my good friend and prayer partner, Sue, listened to me rationalizing.

"I'm not a shrike, am I? Did he just happen to be looking at me?"

Sue remained silent.

The night before, though she's not a drinker, Sue had agreed to go with me into the motel bar to keep me company. Earlier I had consumed the bottle of alcohol I'd brought from home for that week-end seminar. My body demanded more and I asked her to join me in the bar.

She was the only friend in whom I had confided about my alcohol consumption.

For days that minister's words seemed to pound on my wall of denial of any addiction. They penetrated deep into my soul. Finally, I decided that if there was anything hypocritical in me I must allow God to heal me.

Deep inside I knew I had a drinking addiction but on the surface I still denied there was a problem.

The next week I called a more mature Spiritual mentor and made an appointment for her to pray for me. Protective of my addiction, I asked only that she pray for me to be healed if I was a hypocrite. That was how she prayed. She prayed specifically for God to open doors of healing even if I didn't know what they were that day.

Little did I know I had just taken a dramatic life-changing step.

A few weeks later things happened that opened my eyes to my hypocrisy. God was whispering very clearly.

My son-in-law, Dave, a violent alcoholic, went into treatment. When my daughter, Debby, his wife, and I visited him, he handed me his Alcoholics Anonymous Big Book, asking me to read it. Curious, I took it home, wondering why he would lend it to me.

At home I set the book on my dresser and ignored it for a couple of weeks. I wondered if I should read it. After all, it was Dave who had the drinking problem. Surely drinking wine every day was acceptable for Christians.

That was my denial of my addiction. I had switched from bourbon to wine to ease my guilt feelings. After all, Jesus drank wine so that made it okay for me to drink. But Jesus didn't drink over a gallon a day as I did.

Finally, as God whispered, I picked up the Alcoholics Anonymous book and began reading.

Please Stop Praying

It was as if someone had been writing down my thoughts. I read of the shame, self-condemnation and isolation that I was feeling. The writer told of trying to go without a drink for one day, or change from bourbon to wine to control his drinking. I, too, had done that without success. I was shocked.

Like the person writing the story, I thought it was acceptable to drink the remains of alcohol in every glass when I was cleaning up after a party.

The writer said "One full day without alcohol and I went crazy and had to have more drinks than usual." I could say the same thing. Reading it seemed to be the Lord's way of showing me that I might be an alcoholic.

But how was that possible? My mind cranked out all kinds of arguments. I was a Christian and couldn't possibly be alcoholic. Confusion drove me to more compulsive drinking.

The next evening, I met my daughter, Debby and Dave at the rehab facility. He had invited us to their Friday evening meeting.

The rehab director stepped up to the podium to speak. He said, "My name is Father John, I'm an alcoholic." Again God was getting my attention with shocking info. This alcoholic was a priest.

Listening to him, as he told his heartbreaking story, I realized if a priest can be an alcoholic maybe I could too.

He said that the American Medical Association recognizes the disease of alcoholism as a chemical imbalance in certain individuals. He compared it to the chemical imbalance of a diabetic. It's not a matter of weak will power, as I'd thought. He said that alcoholics in recovery are sick people trying to get well, not bad people trying to be good. That helped me to realize I was not a bad person, even if I was alcoholic.

It would take a while for me to admit that I needed to give up alcohol. My addiction kept me confused. I was not yet ready to give up my daily drinking.

Weeks later I finally admitted the addiction to myself. But I was afraid to say anything to anyone about this.

I was married to Sam, a man who had been a heavy drinker since childhood. I felt I had to keep quiet about my new self-awareness.

Divorce would be immanent if I stopped drinking. A few years earlier we had married as drinking buddies. Lately the marriage was becoming shaky.

Even though we'd been married three years, he couldn't seem to understand what it took to be a Christian. Jesus has always been important to me whether I drank or not. So our faith differences made us argue.

Continuing to drink and living in denial a few more weeks, I finally realized it was time for me to stop. I was weary from lying to myself. My behavior was not like a Christian when I was drinking. That was when I'd go to church mentally polishing my halo.

That minister in Moberly was right. I was a "shrike", a hypocrite in denial of my fake walk as a Christian.

My denial ended July 12, 1983. By God's grace I was at the hospital all day caring for my six-year-old granddaughter, while my daughter, Debby, was giving birth to her second son. I was sitting beside her delivery bed when that little head popped out just three feet from me. Those big eyes looked right at me. Suddenly I thought, "I've got to quit drinking!"

That decision became my first day of sobriety. It began on a joyous note.

But the next few days were like hell must be. I was stressed out big time, as I tried to stay sober. I felt like clawing the wallpaper off the walls. Everything in me screamed for a drink.

After four days, I felt I was going crazy. Being married to a serious alcoholic, and keeping my sobriety secret, was shredding me mentally.

Finally, I called my friend Sue.

Sobbing into the phone I blurted, "Sue, that prayer time about whether or not I'm a hypocrite has helped me realize I'm probably an alcoholic. But, I stopped drinking four days ago and I'm going crazy. I don't know what to do."

"Just hang in there," she said quickly, "while I call my Aunt Linda. She's in A.A. She'll call you right away."

A few minutes later the call came in from Sue's Aunt Linda. She understood and told me the story of her battle with alcohol and the joy of her recovery.

Tears of relief streamed down my cheeks. Her words of shame and feeling isolated brought me relief and amazement. I was not alone in what I was feeling. Linda understood.

When she invited me to join her at a meeting of Alcoholics Anonymous, I accepted.

We met at a building that had no signs indicating it was an A.A. hall. And I fearful imagined I'd be in a room with ragged, rough people street bums.

To my surprise I found teachers, office workers, and people like me. They spoke of the same brokenness and self-condemnation I had felt. What they said sounded like what I'd read in the Big Book and had heard from Linda. I could relate so easily. I knew I was in the right place.

Since then I've met people from all walks of life in A.A. They have helped me on my road to recovery.

I was relieved when I heard, and later read in the A.A. book, about a "Higher Power" whom many called God. The twelve steps of the A.A. program emphasize that you cannot get sober and stay sober without that "Higher Power". And we must turn our wills and lives over to Him to stay sober.

My relationship with Jesus Christ became more important than ever when I chose Him over alcohol. I considered the 12-step program an improvement in my "walk" with the Lord. Later I learned that program had been created by a Christian man named Bill Wilson.

Visiting different A.A. groups, I found an interesting variety of people in each one, yet a similarity in format. Some are more accepting of the vocabulary of the active Christian. Some are not. I did hear extreme foul language. But I had to decide to accept it. I learned that acceptance of even foul language is sometimes necessary. Whatever it takes to help a person get sober and stay that way.

Proverbs 23:29-35 describes the illness of alcoholism perfectly. Cautiously, I've shared my faith to individuals in A.A.

So far three people in A.A. meetings have heard me share and asked me how to ask Jesus into their hearts. Then they each asked me pray with them at another location, like their home or mine.

Just a month into recovery, my drinking husband chose to join me in A.A. About a year later, since we had been drunk when we married, that marriage ended. Years later, long after the divorce, he thanked me for helping him get into A.A.

Today I'm grateful for that penetrating look from the visiting minister at Moberly, Missouri, as he spoke of a "shrike".

Beginning my walk to be free from my alcohol addiction was not the healing I expected. But it has healed me of much of my hypocritical attitude. Christ knew what was needed

Chapter #3

The Modern Day Jesus

"..I say to you he who believes in Me, the works that I do he will do also; and greater works than these he will do." John 14:12

    April and I met when she came to my home after calling and asking for prayer. A mutual friend at our church had suggested she contact me. She was a new Christian and willing to come to my home for our prayer time.

    When I open my door that sunny day, I saw a petite beauty, looking very distrustful and frightened. April was about thirty, with a cascade of soft brown curls around her shoulders. Looking into her huge sable eyes, I sensed she was a like a child seeking answers. She was the age of my adult daughter who had a growing family.

    We introduced ourselves and I took her to my living room. Often even new people talk with me easily but April did not. Our initial conversation was stilted with awkward blocks of silence.

    "What kind of work do you do, April?" I asked.

"I'm a secretary at an insurance company."

Then silence. It grew as I searched for another question to help draw her out. The awkwardness made me miss my prayer partner, Linda, who had not been able to join us.

My uneasiness was brief since God's hand was on us. Intercessors were praying elsewhere. Silently I asked Him to break down the barriers. Of course, He did...in a most unexpected way.

April had chosen my recliner when she sat down. Her eyes wandered across the table beside her. Suddenly she snatched up a book lying there.

Beaming with joy she said,"Is someone in your family in A.A.?"

I admitted it was my Alcoholics Anonymous book. The Holy Spirit had done it again, using my weakness to open the door of communication.

April smiled with relief on hearing my positive response. "That's why I'm here," she exclaimed. "I'm involved with an alcoholic and don't know whether to keep helping him or not. He's crippled from a bike wreck. I help him every day. I stop by his place after work. His drinking makes him spout cruel words at me.

Sometimes his anger frightens me. I'm afraid if I get too close to him, he might grab me and hurt me. Sometimes I just want to run out the door. But he needs my help."

As if a flood gate had opened, April's fears and confusion poured out along with words of guilt, and worry. I heard her frustration and sadness.

Years of doing healing prayer had shown me that many people, even Christians, have difficulty believing that God actually heals today. So I respected her fears and quietly tried to follow the Lord's guidance in communicating. I knew He was working in April's life by bringing us together. This was just a step to grow her relationship with Him.

She made use of a nearby box of tissues. Winding down, she wiped away a tear and sighed, "I want to stop taking care of him but he's so helpless. Who'll take care of him? He doesn't have another friend. Just me."

Then she became quiet again.

"You've made a wise choice asking for prayer, April," I said. "The Lord knows just what you both need."

Then I explained about memory healing prayer. At my invitation, she joined me on the couch. I asked if I could put my hand on her shoulder. Looking at me as if relieved by the motherliness in me, she nodded and smiled.

Inviting the Holy Spirit in, I said, "Lord, please show us why April feels she must stay in a destructive relationship, taking care of a man who treats her cruelly. Show us why she feels a strong commitment to this man. Help her to know your wishes in this matter, Father God."

As God whispered instructions, I directed her on a walk back in her memory to her childhood. We took her back to when she was six. Then I asked, "April, did something significant happen when you were about six?"

Her answer came with the voice of a small child, which is common during age-regression prayer.

She said "Yes. That was the year my Mommy was really sick and I had to take care of her."

I prayed for the Holy Spirit to show us what April needed to bring healing.

An image came to me of the child standing beside a bed where her mother lay ill. I asked, "Was your mother so sick she had to be in bed?

Hearing her positive response, I asked, "What are you seeing?"

She described exactly what I saw. God was directing.

In her little-girl voice, she said, "I'm afraid Mommy might die. She gets sick so much and I have to take care of her." She spoke with a pouting tone. Her brow furrowed and her head bowed to hide her tears.

"Describe what you're doing there beside your Mommy," I asked softly.

As she described the scene I pictured her whole house with transparent walls. Tiny April stood beside the bed helping her mother drink a glass of water.

Then I saw Jesus coming up the sidewalk to their front porch. I said, "April, I see Jesus walking up to your house." I described what I saw as He went up the steps, then across to the front door.

But I had to stop, because under his arm I saw a bright red and white bucket of KFC™!

Almost gasping aloud, I silently prayed, "Lord you've got to be kidding! Is that my imagination?"

The Holy Spirit immediately cautioned me to not be rigid but to share the complete picture with April. I was so confused about how I could describe this incongruous scene.

"And. . . " I spoke hesitantly, dragging out the words. "Jesus is holding . . . a bucket . . . of . . . Kentucky Fried Chicken™."

Immediately she clapped her hands. With a joyful grin, in her little girl voice, she piped up saying, "Oh, goody. I have to fix Mommy some supper and Kentucky Fried Chicken™ is my very most favorite."

From that point, God explained to little April how she was keeping others from helping her mother. Thinking she was the sole caretaker, little April believed that sacrificing her own daily needs for a loved one was what she was supposed to do.

Then we saw Jesus come inside the house and take her little hand saying, "April, it's good that you are caring for your Mommy. But if you don't take care of yourself, how can you help her?

You need to eat too, Honey, and you need to let those nice neighbor ladies to come in and help you and your mother.

"April do you want to make your neighbors miss a blessing by not letting them help? You don't have to be a grown up yet. Be the little girl you are and take care of yourself." Jesus said.

Then He told her how proud He was of her.

When we finished praying, her face glowed. She left my home looking very relaxed and satisfied.

Shortly after that, April broke off the friendship with the handicapped man.

She spent the next few years discovering more about herself and building her relationship with Jesus. We often crossed paths at church and would greet each other with a hug.

Eventually she met another man who had a solid military career as an officer. He was handsome and courted her respectfully. After a couple of years they were married in a beautiful wedding. Then she moved far away to where her husband was based. She left behind the problem that had made us friends and she continued to grow in the Lord.

It's still difficult for me to tell the true story of Jesus bringing a bucket of KFC™ to help a girl's memory healing. But He did.

This was how it happened back in the 1980s when I was newly sober and God was bringing many women to me for memory healing prayer.

Chapter #4

Truth Washes Away Pain

"If I then, your Lord and Master, have washed your feet; you also ought to wash one another's feet." John 13:14

If Jerry hadn't been fooling around with other women during our marriage my little girl wouldn't be so messed up today!"

My voice rose in anger as I rationalized about why my daughter Debbie was struggling as a 19-year-old living on her own with her baby.

My good friend Emma listened patiently, as usual, while I dumped my concerns about my kids. Since my two teen-aged sons were still living with me, I kept my anger toward their dad bottled up. I didn't want them to hear me gripe about his infidelity but sometimes I'd just explode when Emma and I were talking about our ex-husbands. I felt the divorce was all Jerry's fault. After all, he was the one who'd had an affair.

My daughter, Debbie, has always been a caring person. Working and putting herself through nursing school, she'd insisted on having her own apartment.

She'd taken in an attractive young man to live with her and her baby.

He was an addict and his seductive skills had won her over. Since he had no job, of course, she was supporting him.

I had asked Emma and other friends to pray for Debbie. I blamed my ex-husband for her poor judgment. My anger toward him expanded to men in general sometimes.

The week after my complaining to Emma, I attended a healing training as part of my church's Healing Prayer Team. Growing spiritually was important to me and I felt blessed to be part of the team.

To properly help others I had to deal with several issues of my own. My marriage ending as it did was my biggest issue. That surfaced when I went to that healing prayer seminar.

Speakers from out of town were teaching about forgiveness. They focused on the importance of copying Jesus.

As professional counseling ministers, they emphasized how we learn best when we first receive forgiveness. Then we are in a position to pass it on. They spoke of how Jesus taught his disciples.

One told about Jesus washing the feet of the apostles and explained why it's important for us to do this. He said that carrying grudges, anger or hatred toward anyone can cause damage to our bodies and souls.

Then he explained in detail how foot washing helps bring healing in those emotional areas.

As he invited us to receive that healing, he said, "Look deep inside yourself. Who has hurt you so badly that you can't forgive? Who is it you may have loved deeply but now hate because of past behavior? Who is it that makes you furious when they come to mind?"

I immediately thought of Jerry. We had been married 15 years when he admitted to an affair with a woman he had been working with.

His revelation threw me emotionally so far off balance that I had a nervous breakdown. I was shattered by the truth that my husband was not who I thought he was. He was a liar and unfaithful.

For two more years we tried to make our relationship work but it deteriorated. Counseling was not even considered. We were low income and had been raised to not discuss family problems with professionals.

The marriage ended.

Here I was, still dealing with my rage five years later at a healing teaching. That evening I became ready to have my anger healed.

The speaker said, "I want you to find someone here to represent that person you think of as your enemy. Then we invite you to wash that person's feet."

He explained the procedure and pointed to the chairs that lined the walls around us in the large meeting room. Each had a basin, a pitcher of water, and a towel. Then he said, "As you wash each foot, tell yourself that Jesus died for this person. Ask yourself what Jesus would be saying while you wash the feet of the offender."

A male friend from my church healing team agreed to sit in for Jerry.

Kneeling before him, I was immediately humbled. I could think of nothing to say as I lifted "Jerry's" left foot and placed it in the basin.

Pouring water over it carefully, I stroked it with my hand. I tried to keep my feelings suppressed, but thinking of Jesus sitting beside me explaining things, brought tears and they began to trickle down my cheek. God was whispering truths to me of the many good things about Jerry.

My love for him surfaced. He had been a good father to our three kids and worked hand in hand with me in parenting. We did well as parents. He had a great sense of humor and was almost always smiling. He was a responsible worker at his job and happy to let me be a stay-at-home Mom.

In spite of their struggles as teens, our kids were becoming self-sufficient young adults.

My anger began to dissolve. I felt grief over the loss of what had once been a good marriage that I had really enjoyed.

Gently I dried his left foot and set it down beside the basin.

As I picked up his right foot, I thought of Luke 7:38 where the sinful woman's tears fell on the feet of Jesus and she mopped them with her hair.

I felt a need to apologize to Jerry for my part in the marriage not working.

Keeping my head bowed to help me believe these were Jerry's feet, I confessed aloud my errors in the marriage. Tears streaking down my face, I admitted my self-righteous attitude and asked his forgiveness.

"Jerry" reached over and patted my head lovingly saying, "You are forgiven." My tears dripped all over his foot. I washed them off.

It seemed Jesus was explaining things and pointing out to me that we had been a good parent team. Jerry had really loved me. He'd expressed his commitment to me by telling me about his affair when he didn't have to. But I had difficulty forgiving him.

Though we tried to hold the marriage together, it was he who filed for divorce a couple of years later.

Drying his right foot, I felt relieved and no longer angry. I had been able to come to terms with the end of a marriage.

The real Jerry had recently remarried, and that evening I began to feel grateful he had found a good mate.

Over the years since then, I've learned much about what causes divorce. Usually both partners blunder.

I had not admitted my share of the problems in that marriage when it was still solid. I had blamed everything on Jerry.

The foot washing opened my eyes to my big issue of feeling everyone else was at fault. I still work on that every day.

That experience helped me in many other ways. It made me aware that I wouldn't have been able to receive memory healing if I hadn't changed churches after our divorce.

My new church helped me grow spiritually. It helped me discover my gift of healing and begin serving. Now, when God guides me through struggles and brings healing experiences, like the foot washing, I'm able use that to help others.

He tells us in 2 Corinthians 1:4 that we are to "pass it on". That has become my lifetime purpose.

Chapter #5

Death Bed Forgiveness

"Verily, verily, I say unto you, except a grain of wheat fall into the ground and die, it abides alone: but if it dies, it brings forth much wheat." John 12:24

    Jenny, and her husband Anthony, were among the first people I met when I started at a new church. Anthony seemed to be constantly frowning when we met. He was a seminary student so I assumed he was just having a bad day. But, over the years, I rarely saw him smile. The corners of his mouth seemed permanently turned down.

    But Jenny was the opposite. She was gentle-natured, often laughing and constantly glowing with the joy of Jesus. She played the guitar and sang with a sweet voice.

    Much as I tried to like Anthony, I couldn't. I didn't even want to be around the guy.

    Jesus tells us to love our neighbor as ourselves. With Anthony that was a stretch.

Finally I realized it didn't mean I had to like him. I just needed to love him as God's kid. It was a struggle but I tried.

Eventually they moved further away in our huge metropolis and I rarely saw them at church.

Several years later I was surprised when I answered my phone and immediately recognized the voice.

"Jenny," I said, "how wonderful to hear from you. I've missed your smiling face at church. How are you?"

"I'm okay," she said hesitantly. It was the first time I'd heard her melodic voice with a serious tone.

She paused, sounding as if choking back a tear, then said, "But right now I have a serious need. Anthony has cancer. We're at the hospital and he's dying. Sally, he asked to have you come and pray for him."

That request, and the fact that her husband was dying, were as unexpected as Jenny's sad tone.

I've never refused to pray for someone when asked. Having done individual praying for many years, I suspected this man's bitterness had eaten at him inside, bringing him to this place of death.

Maybe God planned to do a deathbed miracle. I sensed the Lord telling me to go as quickly as possible.

Of course I did.

But first, I called my young prayer partner, Dave. We arranged to go to the hospital after work that evening.

My own father had lingered near death in a hospital a few years earlier. That caused me difficulty when visiting hospitals. So I was grateful Dave was with me. He seems to always hear God's whisper clearly. I thought of him as another son God sent me as a prayer partner.

Jenny was at the ICU nurses' station when we arrived. She smiled and gave me big hug, then took us to the room where her husband lay, with tubes hanging everywhere.

It was apparent, as we stepped up to the hospital bed, that he would have difficulty talking. A breathing mask covered his face. Yet he gave me a weak smile.

That was a "first".

"Hi Anthony," I said. Laying my hand on his shoulder, I was shocked at how bony he felt.

Quickly I said, "Thanks for inviting us to come and pray for you. Do you have anything specific to want to tell us before we start?"

Grabbing his breathing mask he tipped it up and, with effort, whispered, "I've got someone in my past that I just can't forgive. I don't want to die without forgiving him."

I was touched. Forgiveness is an important step for anyone.

Not wanting to waste any time, Dave and I stepped up to the bed, one of us on each side. Laying hands gently on this dying man, we began to pray using the memory healing prayer we'd done together many times.

I invited Jesus to come and take Anthony for a walk back in his history to where healing was needed. As God whispered, I sensed Jesus taking Anthony back to age eight. Then I asked him, "Did something serious happen when you were eight?"

"He's beating me again," he whispered coarsely as he tipped the breathing mask. In just a few words, he described the scene.

I could see the little boy curled up on the floor. His dad had a belt and was whipping him with the buckle flying against the small body.

"Do you see Jesus there?" I asked. He shook his head.

I continued, "I see Him coming in. He's sitting down on the floor and wrapping His arms around you." Eyes shut and tears rolling down his cheeks, Anthony's face suddenly lit up and he nodded.

I continued to describe what I was seeing. He nodded. Jesus took the next blow of the belt buckle. His dad didn't seem to see Jesus, but suddenly turned and left the room. Jesus continued to hold the boy.

I spoke as the Lord whispered to me. "Jesus says your dad was beating you because he'd been beaten as a child. Your grandpa beat him that same way. That's the only way your dad knew how to keep you from making mistakes he made growing up. But he does love you.

"And, Anthony, Jesus says he's so sorry you have to go through this."

"But, Jesus, can't You see it hurts and cuts me? I don't understand." The voice of the little boy came through the breathing mask.

"My child, did you love Rufus, your dog?" Jesus asked.

"Sure," he replied, nodding.

"Did you have to take a whack or two at him sometimes to get him away from someplace where he shouldn't be?"

Another nod.

Jesus continued speaking through me, "Remember that time he bit into your dad's newspaper? You struck him with your baseball bat to keep him from tearing it up, didn't you? You were really scared and angry. Do you remember that?"

"Yes," the child's voice slowly responded.

"You didn't really mean to hurt him badly did you? But remember how he limped for a long time after being hit by that baseball bat? You never knew you cracked a bone in his shoulder that day did you?"

His young voice of astonishment answered, "No! Did I really hurt him that bad? I was so scared Daddy would be mad; I had to stop Rufus before he tore it up. I had just come home from ball practice and the bat was in my hand."

Jesus said, "Son, that's how your dad usually feels when you do something that could bring serious consequences, or if you've made a big mistake. He becomes frightened of what else you might do. He's trying to save you. Now look at the good you've done with your life."

Anthony was able to see the good honest man he had become. He finally understood and let go of his bitterness and anger.

Listening to Jesus, he realized Christ had shielded him from more blows by keeping him from repeating any mistakes.

Since Jesus understood and loved the Dad anyway, Anthony was able to forgive.

I continued to describe what I was seeing.

As Jesus stood and helped little boy up, both were smiling. Anthony had overcome his fury toward his dad and forgave him.

As Anthony wiped away his tears, my hopes grew for his memory healing. I spoke the words needed to mentally walk him back to the present day.

Relief and satisfaction replaced that scowl I'd always seen on his face. His anger faded.

Once again I was amazed at God's perfect timing. Usually such prayer would take a couple of hours but this one was completed in about twenty minutes. Jesus knew the physical limits that day.

When we left, I asked Jenny to keep me posted on his progress. I truly expected eventual recovery. Two days later she called to tell me Anthony had died quietly the night before.

My first thought was "Oh no. I blew it. What did I do wrong?"

I was so sure he was going to get well.

My confusion melted away with her next statement.

"Thanks, Sally," she said. "Your prayers were just what he needed to bring him closure.

"I've never seen him so peaceful. The Lord cleared his way to heaven."

At the funeral, Jenny again glowed with the joy of the Lord. I'm sure she will keep bringing that joy to others.

And Anthony is at peace.

Chapter #6

God Saves the Rebel

"For I know the thoughts that I think toward you, saith the LORD, thoughts of peace, and not of evil, to give you an expected end." Jeremiah 29:11

"Jim, you know you are not allowed to smoke in our home." I barked my house rule as I stood in our upstairs hallway.

I was about a foot in front of my tall lanky 16-year-old son who held a lit cigarette in his hand.

Mustering up my meanest look, at five-foot-three, my fists on my hips, I felt I was Superwoman. In my mind, though he was six-foot tall, he was still my "little boy".

Suddenly his fist smashed into the wall beside my head, nearly scraping my cheek.

Superwoman was shaken.

Faking bravery, I glared at him and yelled, "That's it! Pack your things and get out! I will not tolerate violence in our home."

He looked at me closely as if questioning my sincerity.

Though shaken inside, I stood firm and angry, hands on hips. My children knew I always meant what I said.

He turned and stomped into his room.

Trembling, I ran downstairs through the living room, to the kitchen, hoping my younger teen, Eddy, would soon be home to protect me. He was as big as Jim, but was at his after-school job.

In a few minutes Jim stomped down the stairs carrying a big bag. He charged out the front door. Stomping across the grass he quickly slid into his car. In tears, I watched from the front window as he threw the bag into the back seat of his blue Chevy Malibu, revved the motor and peeled out.

"Lord," I prayed, "please take care of my son and provide a decent place for him to stay while he deals with this rebelliousness."

That was a new experience for me. As a single Mom, I never imagined I'd have to order my child to leave, much less have him try to hit me.

Yet later that evening I sensed God whisper that I'd done the right thing and I was able to get to sleep trusting God to take care of Jim.

The next morning my phone rang at dawn. Answering, I was relieved to hear the familiar voice of Betty, the mother of Jim's closest friend, Chuck.

"Sally, your son is safe at my home." Betty said. "He's settling into our garage with a cot," she chuckled.

"I just thought I'd call so you don't worry about him. I'll see that he's fed and safe. I'll let you know if anything serious happens. Chuck's glad to have him here. So am I."

I was so relieved. School would be starting in a few weeks. I prayed he'd be home by then so he could complete his senior year. But, I took comfort that he was somewhere safe for the time being.

Though he was going through a violent phase, Jim was born with a talent. He'd always been an excellent artist like both my brothers, who are commercial artists. He also enjoyed writing stories.

Tidying his room, I found notes of Jim saying he doesn't want to live. Frightened, I immediately began praying for his mental health.

Three weeks later the nights began to cool. School was about to start. That's when my wayward boy came home dragging his pride.

I was relieved he was back and had chosen to finish High School. He mumbled an apology and begrudgingly nodded his agreement as I repeated my house rules.

Our time apart had relieved some of our tensions. In the spring Jim graduated, but, classic of the passionate artist, he struggled to do everything his own way.

After graduation he became the manager at the pizza place where he worked. The couple who owned it even invited him to move into their basement apartment.

This time when Jim moved out it was less traumatic, but sad for me. Hugging him, I gave him my blessing and words of love. He returned my hug sweetly, and then said good-bye.

What I didn't know was that he'd inherited an addiction to alcohol. For the next twelve years he worked at the same place and fed his addiction. Though he always attended our family gatherings he was never drunk.

But I couldn't forget his journal I'd found when he was 16, writing about a desire to kill himself. I knew

Please Stop Praying

that alcoholism and suicide are commonly linked. Many times I'd pray, "Lord, you know Jim's needs, his addictions, and his creative good side. Please protect him as he struggles to find himself. Help him to choose to get sober. Help him to know he's loved. Take care of my firstborn son, Lord."

As he neared age 30, Jim became involved with Joann, a girlfriend from his teens. They lived together.

Joann had an evening job so she was gone until nearly midnight. Their relationship was very shaky because of her mental illness.

In December 1987 I prayed, "Lord I know now the danger of daily putting alcohol in our systems year after year. Please, Lord, do whatever it takes to help Jim bottom out and get into recovery."

God heard my prayers. His answer came on January 31, 1988.

At 1:00 A.M. my phone rang. It was Joann. Her voice shook as she said, "Jim tried to kill himself and collapsed inside the house, against our front door.

"When I came home from work I couldn't get in. I finally did and found him unconscious. I called 911 and they rushed him to the hospital. The E.R. doctor said if we'd come in 15 minutes later, Jim would have been dead."

Tears of fear and gratitude spilled down my cheeks as I blurted out. "What hospital? I'm coming right over."

"No. Wait." she said, "They're pumping his stomach and said he'd taken a bunch of pills with lots of alcohol. He'll be unconscious until tomorrow so you don't need to come yet. I'll keep you posted."

Shaken and crying, I hung up thanking God out loud for saving my son.

The next day his boss went to visit Jim and suggested he get in the hospital's alcohol recovery program.

He did.

The doctors wouldn't let anyone visit him until he'd been in been in Rehab a couple of weeks. So, again, I had to wait.

Finally that day came that I could visit. Joann called to let me know. I hung up the phone with a gentle,

"Thank you, Jesus," and hurried to the hospital.

Please Stop Praying

Walking in to the Rehab visitor's room I saw a wide smile on the face of my tall, lanky, Jim. It felt like a miracle had happened. This wonderful, brilliant, talented young man was sober and alive with his old familiar loving smile.

"Hi Mom" he said, opening his arms and giving me a warm embrace.

Usually quiet, he was more talkative and happier than I'd seen him in years. God had His hand on my boy and was bringing a much-needed healing.

I guess God and I both had to wait until Jim was ready to be healed.

Those nice visits continued over the six weeks he was in rehab.

He celebrated his thirtieth birthday there. Two days later he checked out.

Following the rehab director's instructions, he went to an A.A. meeting that day. It was near his home. There he miraculously met with Bob, a strong leader in recovery. I was happy when I learned that. Bob became Jim's A.A. Sponsor. My son developed a solid recovery program.

A few months later my phone rang late one evening. It was Jim. He was at the pizza place where he worked. I was surprised to hear my macho son crying. I'd not known him to cry since he was a child.

"Mom," he whispered through a sob, "all day I've struggled with what Joann said when I left for work this afternoon. She doesn't love me and was moving out.

"I can't handle it, Mama. I think I have to go back to rehab or I'll to do something bad to myself. Can you come and get me from work? I don't trust myself to drive."

This independent son had never asked me for help as an adult. He had not called me "Mama" since he was a child.

I knew God was whispering "Go" and I went with a heart full of gratitude that God was bringing my son more healing.

On the way to the pizza place, driving through the darkness, I prayed for God to show Jim and I, what to do to help him stay alive and make something meaningful of his life.

I had called and alerted the Rehab Clinic giving them his name. It was 11:00 P.M.

I arrived as he was locking the doors to the pizza shop.

Please Stop Praying

As I drove to the hospital rehab he sobbed in grief of losing the only woman he'd ever loved.

The nurse at the Rehab desk surprised us saying that since he hadn't been drinking they couldn't admit him in their facility. But they arranged for him to be admitted to the hospital psyche ward, next door. Jim didn't argue. He knew he needed help.

A week later his smile returned. Every time I'd visit him at the hospital, he talked more sensibly. His stay there wasn't long.

He kept working with his A.A. Sponsor, Bob for over a year. I was delighted later when I learned that Bob was a Christian.

A few months after he left the hospital Jim celebrated his first year of sobriety.

Then he announced he was going to be a commercial artist, like both my brothers.

He left his long-time pizza job and went to school full-time at a local Junior College that had a strong commercial art program.

His married sister, Debbie, and her husband, gave him free room and board in her large home. With her four children he was rarely alone.

So Jim was able to complete the art course and graduate with honors in a year.

By then he had met a new woman and fallen in love. They married and moved out of our home town to his first job as an illustrator.

Ten years later they had a darling baby girl. When their daughter was three, his wife delivered their fine son. Jim keeps progressing in positions as an exceptional commercial artist.

I had no idea of the joyful, amazing changes that would happen in his life, and mine, when God answered my prayers for Jim's sobriety in 1987.

Chapter #7

Forgiveness in Heaven

"You shall not murder." Exodus 20:13

It was a cold autumn day in 1977 when I drove my daughter, Debbie, to a clinic that performed abortions. Our individual thoughts enveloped us in two dark clouds of silence.

Neither of us was willing to speak what we feared God was saying. We had chosen to shut our ears to His voice.

Debbie was twenty, single, and struggling to complete her nursing course at a Vo-Tech school. Two years earlier, she had insisted on leaving home to move to an apartment with her 3-month old baby, Suzie.

With Vo-Tech school, and a part-time job, she struggled financially. Then a young drug addict seduced her and convinced her to let him move in. He introduced her to drugs and led her into a lifestyle that was far from her wholesome upbringing.

Deep inside I cried when I thought of killing a baby in the womb…my grandchild. But Debbie felt it was her only option and I had to respect that.

In a way I was thankful Debbie had chosen to not bring another child into the world. That was the only reason I supported her decision to abort. Everything in me screamed "Stop the car! Don't kill that child in her womb."

But I rationalized, "She's only three months along. This is just an egg. It's not a baby yet."

At the clinic, the solution dripped into Debbie's arm to kill the baby. We said very little. Her mild contractions lasted briefly.

When it was over, the stout gray-haired nurse came back in.

Hands on her hips, like a tough military sergeant giving orders, she reported, "It all went well in spite of the fact that you were five months along, instead of three. It was a little girl."

Inwardly I screamed "No! No! No! We killed a baby girl."

As I drove Debbie back to her apartment, we both held back our tears. Both of us were fighting our guilt feelings and grief. We said very little.

My grief was so intense, within a week I had blocked it off deep inside my head, erasing from my mind the reality of that day.

I forced myself to ignore the overwhelming guilt feelings. I tried to justify our heinous act and get on with my life as if killing a baby had never happened.

Five years later, I was at a Healing Prayer Retreat in Glorieta, New Mexico. It turned out that one of the teachings was about doing Memory Healing prayer around aborted or miscarried babies.

Listening to the speaker, my mind was flooded with suppressed guilt for having encouraged Debbie to have an abortion. My heart was wrenching from my suppressed grief of a lost grandbaby.

Truth surfaced. I was an accessory to murder. Years of silence had become like a thick sheet of ice trapping in my guilt and pain. God's truth was like warm wedges piercing deep inside breaking it loose.

It was time for me to receive healing prayer instead of giving it.

Walking to our cabins after a teaching, I began telling the story to my praying friends, Mike and Nita, and asked them to pray for my horrid memory.

It was a sunny afternoon in Taos, New Mexico.

We found a place to sit outside in the beautiful courtyard. These were friends I'd known a long time. We had been working together on my church Healing Team. I felt safe with them.

They began praying, guiding me back in my memory. The weight of carrying that shame was like a huge sack of ugly rocks slung across my back.

Nita's kind attitude and gentle voice helped me sense them relieving me of the load of guilt. As she prayed she led me back to that day at the abortion clinic.

Instead of the military-sergeant-nurse in the room, there was Jesus. Holding the baby, he said "Sally, this child is safe and loved in heaven now. Would you like to meet her?"

Tears trickled down my face. I was frightened and slow to respond, fearing she would reject me. Then Jesus asked what I had named her.

"Melissa," I said. Suddenly I knew she was a real person and I wanted to see her.

I envisioned Jesus taking my hand. He led me to a delightful playground. It was carpeted in luxurious grass with flowers and colorful playground equipment. Happy children ran and played everywhere.

Pointing to a little girl with long blond curls, He said, "That's your granddaughter, Melissa."

We walked closer.

Swings had always been my favorite place on a playground and Melissa was on one. She looked like Shirley Temple wearing a frilly dress. Then she waved and a beautiful smile filled her face. Jesus introduced us. I watched her chocolate eyes closely. They held no anger or rejection; only joy.

"Hi, Grams," she said in a melodious voice. I was caught off-guard. Melissa's living siblings call me "Grams".

Then she said, "I knew you'd come to see me someday. Will you push me?"

Delighted at her invitation, I said "Of course" and stepped behind her.

I pushed and we chatted about nothing important. Then I sat down in the swing beside her and together we pumped higher and higher, smiling and giggling. After a while we left the swings and walked. Melissa took my hand.

I asked, "How did you know I'd come?"

"Because Jesus is your best friend," she responded simply.

We walked and she told me that she was very happy in heaven because there were lots of kids, and the angels took good care of them.

When we sat down on a park bench I had so much I wanted to say. I cried, "I'm so very sorry, Melissa, that your Mama and I sent you to heaven too soon."

Touching my cheek with her tiny hand, she said, "Grams, please don't feel bad. I know you did the most loving thing you knew to do at the time. I forgive you. Please forgive yourself."

That was what I needed. Forgiving myself was something I didn't know how to do.

Soon it was time to return to the present. Jesus assured me I could come back and visit Melissa anytime.

About a week later, I told my daughter Debbie about that healing prayer time.

She surprised me with a joyful attitude and said, "Mama, while were gone to Glorietta I asked the healing prayer team to pray for me about the same thing. Even though you and I never talked about it, I was also drowning in guilt about that baby.

"God brought me healing too."

That day we held each other and shared healing tears.

Debbie had married that baby's dad, Dave. They had two healthy sons their first three years of marriage. When their younger son was about a year old Debbie and Dave, came to me asking for financial support to abort their third child.

Suzie was ten-years-old and enjoyed being the big sister to the two little brothers.

I explained that I didn't have the money but offered to pray with them.

Debbie knew me well enough that she had actually expected that. I prayed, "Lord, You know what plans You have for this child in Debbie's womb today. We thank you for Suzie and her two healthy brothers. Lord, please help Debbie and Dave know what to do about this baby in her womb."

As Debbie and I cried that day, so did Dave. Later Debbie told me that she had suggested Dave ask me for financial help, hoping I would be able to change his mind. She knew as they left my home that God had just saved her baby.

Six months later Lorie was born. She has been a joyful, loving child. That attitude has continued as she's become an adult. Now, at age 27 she is beautiful, like her sister, and has wisdom beyond her years.

It's as if God helped Debbie and me to rectify our wrong decision 30 years earlier by bringing her three beautiful new children.

As I write this, Lorie is married to a wonderful hard-working man. They have an energetic handsome young son, who's just starting school. Their two-year-old daughter is adventurous and as beautiful as her mother.

Chapter #8

Closing Doors To The Past

"I am the door; if anyone enters through Me, he shall be saved..." John 10:9

She was beautiful. Alice, a petite young mother of a three-year-old was struggling in her second marriage.

At church one Sunday my prayer partner, Linda, graciously listened to her unload her struggles about adjusting to a new husband. Linda, convinced Alice to seek healing prayer. A few days later Linda brought her to my apartment for prayers.

Though he wasn't familiar with my ministry doing healing prayer, my new husband sat reading his newspaper as we went into another room for privacy. This was the first time I was to do praying for someone else in my home. Usually I was at church, receiving instruction and practicing prayer with others on our church healing team.

As the women came in, I could see that Alice was full of sorrow. She wasn't able to look up or smile. She seemed emotionally beaten from her own self-condemnation. Her shoulders sagged. Her head hung low. Her eyes were downcast, as if embarrassed. She sat down slowly on our settee and slumped staring at her hands in her lap. She seemed unable to speak.

"Alice, please tell Sally what we talked about coming over here," Linda said softly, trying to help ease the tension. It was a new experience for Alice.

Finally, accepting those kind words, she lifted her head slightly and began to explain why she had come. Her huge blue eyes filled with tears as she spoke.

"It was about three years ago," she explained, "that I was divorced from Charles, my first husband. He had been unfaithful and wanted out of our marriage. So I took our baby, Donny, and left. I was surprised that the divorce was finalized so quickly."

Her words reminded me of the quick finalizing of my own divorce from the father of my children.

"About a year later", Alice continued, "I met Matt at church. Over time, we fell in love and were married about six months ago. Matt's a wonderful man who's a strong Christian. I know God brought us together, but when we make love, visions of Charles come to my mind. I feel so guilty. I just can't enjoy making love with Matt. So I've avoided it as much as possible. But now Matt wants us to have a baby together."

Alice told how her frustration also caused her to flair up in anger easily. Filled with guilt, she took her anger out on her three-year-old, Donny. Apparently he looked like his birth father, Charles.

That new family's home life was becoming a nightmare, even though it had the ingredients to be wonderful. They wanted Jesus to be Lord in their home.

We talked a while, about what might help resolve the issue. Then we went to prayer. Bowing our heads, I wasn't sure what direction to go with the prayers. But I knew God would know exactly how to take care of the problem.

I invited Jesus to come in and do the healing that was needed. Then we sat waiting quietly with heads bowed.

Linda and I had experienced how God gives one of us words or a vision. He did, by whispering some truths to Alice.

"Do you see anything, Alice?" I asked.

She said, "I'm seeing myself with Jesus beside me. We're kinda up in the clouds beside an open door."

She sounded puzzled.

I quickly explained "Jesus often helps us close doors on the past. That must be what He's showing you today."

As Alice spoke, Linda and I were both able to see the open door. It stood by itself in what looked like the clouds of heaven.

Jesus stood beside Alice as she looked through the open door. His arm was around her shoulders. She had her hand on the doorknob and was looking out at her former husband, Charles.

He stood about 40-feet away, with his back to them. Two angels stood beside him.

Speaking as the Lord guided, I asked Alice, "Do you trust Jesus to take care of Charles?"

She was hesitant to answer.

As Christ whispered His words of guidance, I asked, "Are you willing to close that door, Alice?"

The door was to her past. For Alice to receive the needed healing it had to be closed.

Many times the Bible mentions doors as a symbolic way to our hearts.

Alice was obviously not ready to close that door. "I don't want to. I can't. I love him," she sobbed with embarrassment.

We listened for several moments as she tortuously poured out her feelings and frustrations. Then she received words of assurance from Jesus. I spoke His words as I heard them. Jesus made it clear that she was not guilty of unfaithfulness to Matt by remembering Charles. They had created a child together. That gave them a bond that made it more difficult for her to close the door since ending the marriage had not been Alice's choice.

Because she had accepted God's gift of Matt as her husband, it was time to close the door on Charles. Jesus explained that her healing could only come when she chose to let go of the past, to close that door and embrace her present life. Jesus assured her that the joy, love and peace she'd been searching for with Matt would come when the door was closed.

We waited patiently in silence as Alice battled her feelings. She seemed to take a long time. I began to wonder if she'd ever close that door. She did have the right to choose.

After a while, with difficulty and tears, she finally did close the door.

There was nothing we could have said to persuade, or hurry, her. We could only wait. She had to make that choice. And she did.

Closing the door slowly in the vision, she told us about each step as she made her choice. Finally the latch clicked shut. Then, with reluctance, she released the handle.

God gave me the vision of Charles and the angels in the distance.

I explained what I saw happening. "I see Charles, and he's getting farther away, Alice. Those two angels are tending to him as he turns and walks away. Please remember that he never turned toward you as we saw him far away."

She bowed her head and grabbed another tissue to catch her tears. Those tears had become her acceptance of God's healing.

Then I told her how I was seeing Matt, her handsome new husband, standing beside her at her door.

He looked down on her with love in his eyes.

Hearing that, Alice suddenly said to Matt in the vision, "Honey, I apologize for not letting go of my past with Charles. I was holding onto the man that I thought he was. During healing prayer I realized my memory was not true. Jesus showed me the truth. Charles really didn't love me. So I chose to let him go, with all the false memories.

"I'm free of the fake Charles who I thought I had married. I hope you'll forgive me. I'm so grateful God helped us meet at church. Today I choose to be your wife forever. Please forgive me."

In our vision, Matt immediately embraced her, and kissed her lovingly, saying, "There's nothing to forgive. Let's just keep moving forward."

Jesus stood beside the couple embracing them. Because Alice loved Jesus first, she had been hearing Him and making good decisions. Jesus completed her healing.

When she raised her head as we closed the prayer time, Alice's face was completely changed. She beamed with joy, like a woman in love.

Walking out the door, her back was straight and her head held high. She turned and we hugged goodbye, and she said she felt a deeper love for Matt than she had ever felt before. She was radiant.

Walking out to the car, Alice and Linda chatted joyously. Her transformation came from being freed from guilt, by letting go of the past.

Every time I saw her after that she was radiant.

Nine months later, Alice gave birth to Matt's first child, a baby girl. What a delightful symbol of God's healing touch.

Chapter #9

Unbeliever is Healed

"At that time Jesus answered and said, 'I thank thee, O Father, Lord of heaven and earth, because thou hast hid these things from the wise and prudent, and hast revealed them unto babes.'" Matthew 11:25

"Now, Sally, keep an open mind. Delores is a fine woman even though she was brought up in a witch's coven."

My buddy Georgia's bubbly voice was cheerful as usual. As I drove slowly past all the beautiful lakeside homes, Georgia tried to prepare me for her friend. This was my delightful prayer partner who always looked for the good in others. But she was taking me to my first experience being around a person raised in a very different way than either of us had ever known.

Gabby Georgia explained how amazingly she had met and bonded with this woman. Since Georgia is so loveable and, lightheartedly comical, I could easily understand.

And I was aware of a sense of tremendous peace around the fine modern lakeside home as we arrived.

That surprised me. This was the home of a woman raised with evil, so her peaceful home puzzled me. It seemed a contradiction.

When she answered the door I admired her elegance. Her outfit was casually dignified. She stood and walked erect like royalty, which I hadn't expected. With her neat gray hair pulled back into a bun, she wore an expensive designer shirt over stylish slacks.

Despite the elegance, I could see anguish in her eyes. I liked her and was pleased that she seemed to feel the same.

Georgia had told me, as we drove over, that Delores' parents had taken her to satanic rituals in the woods where the people wore hoods as they danced and did demonic things. She had been sexually abused there as a child. She'd been taught that it was Biblical.

At home her father had yelled and pounded the Bible to make a point sometimes. It made her hate the Bible and anything that was said about it.

When Georgia first called asking me to come and pray for Delores, she had told me some of this.

In preparation for that day, she and I had fasted for a week. I'd also asked intercessors to be praying. Since I use the name of Jesus frequently during healing prayer I was concerned that it might cause problems with Delores. What if she suddenly told me to leave before the Lord could touch and heal her?

I was concerned, not knowing what to expect in dealing with a woman with her background.

Talkative Georgia surprisingly grew quiet as we entered the house. Yet I sensed a sweet spirit of Jesus there. It seemed someone had to have been praying for some time around that home. Delores led us into her finely furnished living room. We settled on the couch and she left to bring us cups of coffee. Her attitude was pleasant, though reserved.

When preparing to pray with someone I don't know, I usually take my time and listen.

Through the living room window the view of the huge lake helped me absorb the peace of the Lord.

When Delores settled into a nearby chair after serving us, she turned toward me and abruptly said, "I don't know that I believe all this 'Jesus stuff' but I have known Georgia for years and she says Jesus loves me and that you can help relieve my anguish over my bad memories.

I had become virtually shockproof over the years but her openness caught me by surprise. My tensions

slipped away, bringing a smile of relief to my face.
I said, "You're very wise, Delores. Georgia's a good person to trust. I've often envied her child-like joy. It seems the love of Jesus always shines through her."

Obviously the intercessory pray-ers were being heard in heaven.

This woman's openness gave me the courage to say, "I have to admit, I've been trying to figure out how to pray without offending you. I often say the name of Jesus."

She smiled and said, "Actually I had expected that. But I'm 54-years-old and have been angry with Jesus all my life. In psychotherapy when I remembered some of the rituals of my childhood, they reminded me of painful memories.

"Now as I've become friends with Georgia, I am confused about Jesus. I was taught that he's an angry person if we don't do things his way. But now I'm hearing that he loves me.

"How could he let those things happen to me as a child if he loved me?

"Still, Georgia insists that Jesus loves me so I finally agreed to have you come and pray for me.

Hearing either of you say 'Jesus' isn't as painful I thought it would be."

From there our conversation came more easily. The tension seemed to be defused. I encouraged her to talk and she told us more about the ritual sexual abuse and demands that her parents made as they pounded on a Bible. For nearly an hour we talked. I nodded my understanding and her tears came as if she was relieved that someone heard her.

Finally she became quiet and said "I'm ready for you to pray."

I said, "Thank you so much for sharing all of that, Delores."

Then I explained how we would be praying, assuring her that Jesus loved her then and knew exactly what she needed that day.

Like a trusting child, she nodded, that she understood. Then she dabbed her tissue at another tear. Such trust was not what I expected with someone from that kind of background.

Georgia helped her move to the couch so she could sit between us as we prayed.

Bowing our heads, I said "Come, Lord Jesus, and bring Delores the peace she needs". Then I invited the

Holy Spirit to take her back in her memory to her childhood where she needed His healing touch.

I had expected we would go to a place in her memory where she had been molested. Instead God directed us to go all the way back to her birth.

Once again Jesus showed us His loving power in a new way through the birth process with memory healing prayer.

I described the vision I was receiving. It was in a hospital delivery room and Delores was coming out of her mother's womb.

With a joyous grin, Jesus received the tiny baby as she emerged from her mother. In his big hands he lifted her up saying

"Look, Father. Isn't she beautiful?"

Angels surrounded Jesus expressing their joy, singing and clapping.

Jesus held baby Delores as nurses cared for her mother. He wiped her tiny face with a soft clean cloth. Love sparkled in His eyes. He lifted her to his lips and tenderly kissed her chubby cheek.

As I described what I was seeing, all three of us were sniffling and reaching for tissues. The depth of Christ's love for Delores touched all our hearts.

We lingered on that loving scene several minutes, soaking in the love and praise that Jesus and the angels gave for one tiny new baby.

I later learned that was exactly what Delores needed so she could believe that Jesus really loved her.

I was surprised Jesus did not take us to painful memories of abuse. Going to that happy time enabled Jesus to show Delores how happy he was about her birth. That helped her receive His love. She needed such an experience that day. Jesus knew. I didn't.

To close the prayer time, I told Delores "Now we're going back through your childhood, young adult time, and to the present time today." I spoke slowly, as God whispered.

We mentally came back to the present time and closed the prayer.

As God often gives Scripture quotes, I wrote one down for Delores to look up. It was Psalm 139. Then, with hugs all around, Georgia and I left.

Delores stood at her door waving to us, her face aglow knowing she is truly loved.

A week later she called and told me that before I came to pray for her, she had seriously considered suicide. After Georgia talked her into getting prayer, she had postponed that.

Delores sounded in awe as she told me that when we prayed she had been amazed that Jesus knew how to give her just what she needed. Hope. That hope turned her in another direction.

That simple vision, of Jesus kissing her cheek, touched her soul and brought emotional healing beyond my comprehension.

Only Christ could have known how to bring that healing.

A few weeks later, Delores called again. "I want you to know," she said, "I purchased a Bible. I can't get the memory from my mind of Jesus kissing my cheek when I was born."

She sobbed, saying, "I still have difficulty believing He really loves me. But I want to know Him better. I think reading the Bible is the best way.

"Thank you, Sally, for helping me see that 'I am fearfully and wonderfully made'*."

*Psalm 139:14

Chapter #10

Healing Priority to Babies

"Call on me and I will answer you and show you great and mighty things you know not of."   Jeremiah 33:3

"Oh, Sally, Ken and I need you. We're at the hospital with our baby, Mindy Sue."

My friend Katy's voice trembled as she spoke of her darling six-month-old daughter. Katy and her husband Ken were my friends from church.

Her tearful words were choked with her sobs as she continued, "She's so tiny and she has encephalitis.

The doctors say she's not going to last long. They have her in an incubator. I guess she's susceptible to every germ imaginable.

She concluded by asking, "Please get a prayer team notified and come here to the hospital ASAP.

"Please, please come and pray over our sick baby girl."

Motivated by a dying baby, I immediately called Marcia, then Dave, my prayer partners. Thankfully they were both available to meet me at the hospital in an hour. Then I called an intercessor and asked her to get her team praying.

I'd heard of encephalitis but didn't know much about it. So, quickly as I could, I read about it and learned that it's an inflammation (irritation and swelling) of the brain, usually caused by infections. But many times doctors weren't sure exactly what did cause it.

Twenty years ago, when this call came, there was little they could do except keep the patient comfortable when dying.

Marcia, Dave and I each lived a few miles apart, in three different directions, in metropolitan Kansas City. We agreed to meet in the foyer of the huge hospital so we could pray together before we met with Katy in the Pediatric Ward.

I was curious about why I did not sense any real urgency, in spite of the mother's frantic plea.

An hour later, when we reached the Nurse's Station of that ward, Katy was waiting for us.

"I'm so glad you all came. Mindy Sue is in there," she said, pointing to a window of one of the rooms.

The baby was so tiny she could hardly be seen in the incubator. It was arranged so the nurses could watch all the babies from their central station.

Standing beside the incubator were two men wearing surgical masks. One was Katy's husband, Ken, who watched the doctor put his hands into the incubator to examine Mindy Sue.

"I don't know what's happening," Katy said,"but the doctor arrived just a few minutes ago. When I asked him what was going on, he didn't say anything except that the nurse had called him and he needed to examine her. I'm so scared."

Sobbing, she turned to me crying. I reached out my motherly arms and embraced her. She was the age of my daughter.

Taking a deep breath to quiet her sobs, Katy stepped back and continued. "I guess after the doctor comes out its okay for two of you to go to the Scrub Room. That's where you can put on the hospital gowns and masks so you can go in and pray over Mindy Sue. But you'll need to wait until the doctor leaves."

As she spoke, she pointed to the closet-type place between the hallway and the baby's room. Windows filled the upper part of both doors. One door went into the tiny Scrub Room and the other went into the larger room where the incubator was.

As Katy was talking, the doctor came out and walked quickly toward her. She directed Marcia and I into the room to change into scrubs. Then she hurried over to hear what the doctor had to say.

Our prayer partner, Dave stayed at the Nurse Station beside Katy to hear the doctor's report. Marcia and I helped each other tie the gowns in the back, over our street clothes. Quickly we sat on the benches putting on the shoe covers, and then head covers.

When we stepped into the room with the baby, we looked through the window at the doctor talking with Katy, who was smiling.

With his face-mask off the doctor seemed very excited. The nurses were smiling. So were Katy and Dave. One nurse was slowly shaking her head in dismay as she grinned.

Ken was walking toward us removing his mask. I was surprised to see him grinning and removing his mask.

Joyfully, he exclaimed, "She's healed!"

Marcia and I stood in amazement as he explained. "The doctor said he's never seen encephalitis heal this quickly. Her swelling is completely gone.

"But he wants to keep her in the incubator and watch her for a couple of days to be sure she is well. He says we'll have to maintain the usual precautions."

He grinned broadly then said "Praise God!"

Macia and I echoed his praise.

Smiling and shaking his head in amazement, Ken continued. "I could tell something good was happening while the doctor was examining her. I could see his smiling eyes above his mask."

Then, Ken put his hand on my shoulder and said, "Please go ahead and pray since you drove out here. We can't have too much prayer."

When we finished praying, he went on to explain. He and Katy had watched from the hallway when the nurse went in to give Mindy Sue an injection. It was right after Katy had called me.

Obviously, the nurse had noticed something that caused her to lay the syringe aside and examined the baby. Then she had left quickly and called the doctor.

"All I saw was her eyebrows raised like she was surprised. Then she smiled."

Ken was grinning as he told us. "I thought that was a good sign since I hadn't seen the nurse smile in a couple of days. I guess I was right," he said with a comical grin as he looked at his tiny daughter.

When we returned to Katy's side she was listening to the nurse as she explained that the smiling baby caused her to check a few crucial places.

That's when she had hurried out to call the doctor. Not wanting the parents to get their hopes up she kept silent about the healing she suspected. She wanted doctoral verification first.

That came when the doctor's examination brought the same conclusion. The nurse explained they were going to keep the baby under observation for another twenty-four hours to be sure she was total healed.

"It's a miracle," the nurse said, in a soft voice with a wide grin.

We knew she was right. Evidently God had touched and healed the baby as soon as Katy called and asked for help. That's why I felt no urgency.

We were all ecstatic, praising God out loud.

Before we left, we watched Katy enter the baby's room wearing the scrub garb.

What a joy to see little Mindy Sue grinning up at her mother when she heard her familiar voice. That child is blessed with parents who know they serve an awesome God.

Chapter #11

A Battle With Darkness

"And certain women, which had been healed of evil spirits and infirmities, Mary called Magdalene, out of whom went seven devils..." Luke 8:2

"The class on Deliverance is about to start in the sanctuary." The speaker made the announcement as a block of classes were ending.

I was thrilled to be in Anaheim, California, at John Wimber's church. Several of us, from the healing prayer team at my church in Kansas City, had arrived four days earlier for this conference.

Deliverance was not my favorite topic when learning about how to do healing prayer, but it is necessary.

I have to admit, that day I considered whether or not to attend that class. I just wanted to take a break after several days of soaking in teachings. This was the last session before my prayer team headed back home to Kansas City.

I was exhausted. The conference leaders had offered a variety of subjects all week. But, at that moment, I felt I needed to sleep to fill the two hours left before we were to leave for the airport to fly back home.

Finally I decided to go into the main sanctuary where they were holding the Deliverance class, and just take a nap near the back.

But that speaker's powerful voice was hard to ignore. What he was saying caught my attention.

"Do you know there's power in the name of Jesus?" he thundered. "Demons are not as strong as many people think."

I was hooked, and chose to skip a nap.

He continued, "They run at the sound of the name of Jesus. Demonic possession inside someone is not common, as many people think. Most dark spirits hang around outside of people and speak lies into their ears to control them. Jesus gives us the power to evict those spirits of darkness."

Scribbling notes frantically on the handout sheet, I realized fear was why I'd avoided teachings on this subject. I had difficulty believing that saying the name of Jesus would give us power against demons.

Then he told this story. "My wife, Sue, was closing the door after our son ran inside our home, fearful of a large teen boy who had just threatened him. I wasn't home yet.

"Suddenly the angry teen, outside, headed up our front walk toward our house. Sue was obvious as she stood behind the glassed-in storm door. She knows the power and protection the Lord gives us, so she barked, 'In the name of Jesus Christ I order you to leave.'

"The teenaged boy was about 15 feet from the door where Sue was clearly visible.

He stopped abruptly, threw his cigarette down, turned, and walked briskly to his pick-up. He climbed in and peeled out as he drove away. He could not have heard her, yet the Lord turned him around."

"I can do that," I thought, though I had no experiences in ordering demons around.

According to this teaching, God gives us power by simply speaking as the Bible tells us. That teaching made me excited to know more.

The speaker went on to tell about wearing the whole armor of God, as told in Ephesians 6. He spoke also of the power of "pleading the blood of the Lamb," as in Revelations 7 and 12.

He said, "Quoting God's words are strong instruments of battle. Since demons are spiritual, it takes God's words to knock them down.

"Study John 14:12-14 where Jesus tells us if we ask the Father anything in His name, it will be done, if we love Him and follow his commandments."

These simple teachings from this man were amazing me.

"If you are confronted by a demon when praying over someone, you can say 'Spirit of darkness, you no longer have power over this person because of the shed blood of Jesus Christ. In the Name of Jesus, I order you to leave.'

"Demons are quickly evicted when you say those words out loud. That's very important. Do not just think about those words. Do not speak them softly. Speak them with authority; the authority that Jesus gave us as He hung on the cross and died."

He went on to explain that since spiritual warfare is not a popular subject, most ministers keep a low profile about it. But it must be taught since evil moves in secretly and appears unexpectedly anywhere. There are existing witch covens everywhere.

To lighten up those dark facts, the minister added that we balance battling with darkness by joyfully praising and worshiping Jesus Christ.

My two hours in that class flew by. I kept taking notes. When the closing prayer came I was invigorated.

On the way to the airport with other members of our team, I couldn't contain my excitement. As we flew, I shared the teaching at that class with my friend Cindy.

She and I had been roommates all week.

As I repeated the teachings I'd heard, my mind seemed to lock in on them. Cindy also became interested in what I'd just learned, and asked questions.

When I arrived in at my home in Kansas City, I unloaded my luggage. Then I hurriedly left for the house of Elaine, a young woman from church.

A week earlier, Elaine had asked me to pray for her the evening when I returned from California.

I had enlisted a team of intercessors but didn't take a prayer partner with me. I usually do, but Elaine seemed to have a simple need, from what little she had told me.

Praying as I drove, with the deliverance teaching fresh on my mind, I added a plea for the Blood of the Lamb to be over us for protection. I had just learned that.

At her house, Elaine welcomed me with a smile and we sat down to chat over iced tea.

I gave her a brief rundown of my trip but avoided mentioning details of any classes.

After several minutes of catching up, I smiled and asked, "What is it you need prayers for tonight, Elaine?"

"What I want," she said in her soft voice, "is for more self-confidence. Something inside me keeps telling me I'm no good. So, even though there are some things I want to do, and learn, I just don't try. I'm starting to get depressed and lacking energy. I even need friends to help me clean my house."

Feeling confident it would take a simple prayer, I said, "OK, let's take it to the Lord and see what happens."

We sat side by side on the couch so I could give her a comforting touch as needed.

I began by inviting the Holy Spirit to come, bringing healing. Then we waited as I listened for the

Lord's guidance. I asked Elaine if she sensed God saying anything?

"God won't say anything!" came her reply, in a deep ugly male-sounding voice.

An eerie feeling hit me, mingled with shock. Immediately I recognized the problem was an evil spirit. My mind was fresh from the teachings I'd just received.

So, I spoke firmly, with authority, saying, "Spirit of darkness, in the name of Jesus Christ I order you to leave."

"I don't acknowledge that name." Again the gravely evil voice came from lovely Elaine.

I looked at her. She was scowling at me. Her blue eyes were dark and glared with the bad spirit.

Speaking more loudly with authority, as I'd been taught, I commanded, "The blood of Jesus Christ was shed to break your power over Elaine.

"In the name of Jesus I order you out!"

The dark spirit left immediately.

The distortion on Elaine's face, and the dark in her eyes changed instantly.

Tears of relief started streaming down her face. Her mouth fell open as if stunned. Her bright blue eyes sparkled clearly.

Frankly, I was surprised with how quickly and easily the dark spirit left.

We closed the prayer and I asked the Holy Spirit to stand guard against any more spirits of darkness trying to enter Elaine.

I said "Amen!"

Then she threw her arms around me, with tears of joy as she bubbled with gratitude.

"Thank you so much, Sally. I didn't know how to explain what was bothering me. I knew the Lord would tell you what to do and say."

Amazingly all of that happened in about 15 minutes. I shook my head in wonder as I told her about the teaching I "just happened" to attend that afternoon.

I've not had another experience like that since. It was one of the most powerful prayer times I've ever done. Needless to say, God's timing was perfect, as always.

I'm still amazed how He brought me a teaching that day and I had avoided it all week. That made it fresh on my mind when I met with Elaine. How much more caring could our God be?

For months afterward, when Elaine and I saw each other at church she made a point of coming to tell me that the dark spirit had not returned.

She became involved with church groups and no longer needed help cleaning her home. Her blue eyes sparkled consistently.

At last, Elaine had found her peace and joy. We both had an unusual experience seeing the true power of the name of Jesus.

Chapter #12

Smiles Covering Pain

"Woe to the world because of offenses! For offenses must come; but woe to that man(woman) through whom the offense comes!" Matthew 18:7

"Hey, Sally, are you going to lunch?" Aaron's strong voice, from across the hall, brought me to a halt. I had just opened the church door to leave after services one Sunday.

As usual Aaron was grinning widely. I let the door close and stepped back inside to wait for him.

Returning his smile, I nodded, "Sure, I'm starved. Where are you going, Aaron?"

I admired this young man because he persevered in spite of a serious birth handicap. He'd keep on keeping on, always with a bright smile, although every move was difficult for him.

With the help of his forearm crutches, he made his way toward me. His legs had limited movement yet he managed to semi-drag them along. Cerebral palsy from birth had limited him physically.

But there was no limit to his infectious smile, his outgoing personality, or his zest for life.

"We're going to the Salad Bar. Want to join us?" he asked.

I quickly agreed as I saw two other single friends, Sharon and Tony, coming toward us. The four of us were close, sharing our joys and sorrows as singles. I enjoyed their company.

We left after deciding who would drive to a favorite nearby restaurant. Our laughter filled the afternoon making my sides ache by the time we left. Returning to church, we split up, each heading for our own vehicles.

Then Aaron called out to me, "Sally wait! Please."

He grinned briefly, looking like he was trying to figure out how to word something.

I waited.

"Sally," Aaron said hesitantly, "Would you do some healing prayer with me next week. I've got some old anger and other stuff I need prayers for."

"Sure, Aaron," I answered. "We can use a room here at church. I'll ask Dave to join us. He's my prayer partner."

His beaming smile returned.

Looking relieved, he quietly said, "Thanks Sally." We hugged good-bye, then parted for our homes.

I arranged for my prayer partner, Dave to join us and for other intercessors to be praying from their homes.

The nextSunday morning, during my daily prayer, I asked "Lord, please move through Dave and I when we pray with Aaron. Help us put our feelings aside to do Your will. We don't know what he needs, Lord, but You do. Your will be done, not ours. Thank you, Lord, for this opportunity to help someone."

After church the three of us met in a counseling room.

When Aaron began to explain what he wanted I was a little surprised. I had actually thought he'd ask for physical healing. But he didn't. He asked for memory healing to forgive his mother's cruelty toward him as a child.

Having accepted his physical limitations, for many years he'd bottled up anger toward his mother. As he asked for prayer, he only mentioned that she had treated him cruelly in his childhood, without giving any specifics.

When we do memory healing prayer, our lack of knowledge of the person's exact need is actually good because we know God will bring what's needed. The less we know the better, sometimes.

As we began, I prayed for the Lord to lead Aaron back in his memory where he needed to be healed. We went back a couple of decades taking him to age eight.

When I asked him what incident with his mother came to his mind at that age, Aaron told us what he saw. From his front porch, he was trying to walk alone down the high steps. The leg braces were new and awkward for him, but he was determined.

"Mama's yelling again," he said, almost in tears as if he were eight at that moment.

"She wants me to go down the stairs on my own, but she's impatient. I want to try it. But she's standing behind me and doesn't think I can make it alone. She always carried me.

I know I can do it but she's yelling at me to hurry up. I can't figure out how to start since I've never done it before."

Dave and I each visualized this as he told it.

Aaron's little child's voice was filled with anguish and frustration as he spoke of his mother's rage and her cruel words.

Then, overcome with anger, she suddenly pushed him.

My own motherly feelings rose to fury, wanting to scream to protect that child. But long ago I learned to banish such thoughts when praying with someone.

As God whispered, I envisioned myself putting my anger in a bag and handing that to Jesus. I'm grateful I was able to do it quickly that day. I couldn't imagine a mother doing what Aaron's mother had done. But we knew God was working.

Taking a deep breath, I asked, "What do you see, Aaron?"

"I'm lying on the sidewalk," he said. "My head hurts, I put my hand on it and it feels wet. I look at my hand and it's bloody and it makes me cry."

Speaking in the child's voice he was getting choked up.

"Where's your Mama, Aaron?" I asked softly.

"She's up on the porch and looks shocked."

I continued to probe gently, "Aaron, can you see Jesus?"

"Uh Huh," he mumbled with a nod.

"Where is He?"

In a childish whisper, he said "He's sitting beside me on the ground, with his hand on my shoulder telling me Mama's afraid. That's why she gets so mad at me.

She's afraid I'll get hurt. She's afraid she'll be late. She's afraid of lots of things. That's what makes her get so mad.

"But, Jesus is saying Mama loves me," he spoke as if he was really there.

"Oh! There's Mama hurrying down the stairs with a towel. She's dabbing at the blood on my head. Now she's picking me up and running to the car with me. Jesus is running with us. Mama's crying. I don't remember ever seeing her cry."

"She drives me to the hospital. We're there a long time. But now I see Mama driving us home. She's crying when she tells me she's sorry she pushed me. In my bedroom with my brother, she lays me in my bed and

Please Stop Praying

fluffs pillows under my head. Then she tells me again that she's really sorry. I guess she does love me, like Jesus said."

He finished his story with a weary smile.

Then he began adding more, "But the next time I wanted to try walking alone down the steps, Mama yelled at me again and scolded me.

"She just picked me up and carried me down, mad like always. But I know she loves me 'cause Jesus said so.

"And she even tells me she was sorry for pushing me all those times before."

Aaron seemed at peace with that new information from Jesus and words from his mother.

We agreed it was time to return to the present.

In our closing prayer Dave asked the Lord to bring Aaron the peace he needed. Taking a deep breath and through his thick glasses I could see a tear in the corner of Aaron's eye.

"I'd forgotten that Mama said she was sorry. I needed that. And Jesus telling me Mama was afraid. I'd never thought about that.

"I guess anger is her only way of dealing with her fears," He said, and seemed at peace about the prayer time.

We talked a little longer. I suggested he read Psalm 139.

Then Dave and I walked him out to his truck that was adapted for his physical limitations. We watched while his strong arms heaved his body inside. We both smiled with affection for this courageous friend.

As we walked to our own cars, Dave and I talked about our frustrations and anger at Aaron's mother.

Before we parted, we prayed that God would continue to bring Aaron peace and healing of his anger.

Then Dave prayed for Jesus to take our anger and bring us both peace.

The next Sunday, Aaron talked lovingly about his mother. He even began to enjoy his visits with her as she mellowed out in her golden years.

Now in his fifties, Aaron continues to share his ever-ready smile and delightful sense of humor. He seems to love his mother and be at peace with the mended broken memory.

Chapter #13

Poison Ivy Healed

"Ask and it shall be given to you..." Matt. 7:7

"Mama, I just got back from the dermatologist and he says I've got the worst case of poison ivy he's ever seen."

Eddy's voice, over my office telephone, tore at my heart. The youngest of my three children, he was fifteen and had just spent a week helping clear ground at a church camp.

Since his dad and I divorced three years earlier, I was hoping my ex-husband would see that our two sons were going to church. During that summer, I was pleased when Eddy announced he'd be going to help build a church camp for teens.

But that day I was so disappointed that he had come home with bad news. Instead of joy and excitement about having a fun experience he had this horrid case of poison ivy.

He'd always been sensitive to poison ivy but this turned out to be his worst case ever. I was bitter and confused, questioning why God had let him get this torturous rash that week.

Such severe reactions had plagued him all his life. When he and his older brother, Jimmy, were younger, they enjoyed playing along the creek behind our home. I took time to teach them both how to recognize and avoid poison ivy.

But, of course, adventurous little boys don't always think about such practical things when exploring the woods. Consequently for about ten years, at least twice a year Eddy would have to suffer with severe poison ivy.

The first time he broke out with it I could tell it was not normal. That began many trips to the doctor. Our family doctor had sent us to a dermatologist who told us that Eddy has an unusually strong allergy to that plant and would always need to see the doctor for special treatment.

What was worse was that each time he had it he took longer to heal. Even the specialist was puzzled by that unusually long time. Most people heal in ten days or so. Eddy had always battled it three or four weeks.

That day, when Eddy called me at my office to report his worst case ever, I sensed he had reached his limit and was ready to be done with poison ivy. We all were. But how do you stop it?

After talking with him several minutes, I asked, "Could Debbie and I come over after I get off work and pray for you?"

"Sure! It can't hurt." he responded. I was surprised since he had never been interested in healing prayer.

His seventeen-year-old sister, Debbie, and I had been attending a new Charismatic church where we were learning healing prayer. We were excited and hoping for an opportunity to practice what we'd been taught.

I was relieved, and surprised, when he agreed.

Since the divorce, my sons had lived with their father in a condo near my townhouse complex. Their father had no interest in growing spiritually, and didn't want to be around me.

That day Debbie came in from school just as I arrived home from work. I told her about Eddy, and that he was willing for us to come and pray.

With a joyful smile, she jumped into my car right away and we headed over to the guy's condo. I drove praying out loud that we could complete praying for Eddy before their dad came home.

Please Stop Praying

When I'd parked, Debbie hurried up to the front door and knocked, with me close behind.

Eddy has always been an exceptionally good-looking young man, and had thick curly blond hair. I enjoyed watching young girls turning to smile at him. I'd never thought about the possibility of my son not looking attractive. But that day I learned it was possible.

When Debbie knocked, my thoughts were of my "baby" being in pain. I braced myself for the worst.

Nevertheless, I was not prepared for the distorted creature who opened the door. My tall, handsome son looked like a monster from a horror movie. He stood there in cut-off jeans only, literally covered from head to foot with itching, red, cracked, oozing sores. Even his lips and face were swollen and distorted with the infectious crusts. His eyes were swollen partially shut and coated with the scales.

He held his arms out from his body since it reduced the pain in his infected armpits. Covering his chest, shoulders, arms and legs everywhere, were red flaky blotches seeping their poison. I choked back my disgust and tears.

Hoping to bring him quick relief with prayer, Debbie and I stepped into the foyer beside him.

I was thankful he was home alone since his dad probably would not approve of our praying. His brother, Jimmy, was at work at the local pizza place.

Eddy suggested we just stand and pray in the foyer.

When we reached to lay our hands on his muscled shoulders, Eddy instantly recoiled.

"Don't touch me! You'll get it!" he warned loudly, trying to protect us.

"No, Honey," I said sweetly, "We're shielded. We're safe because the Bible said so."

We had recently been taught Luke 10:19 which tells how God gives us authority so we will not be hurt when we are serving Him. We knew God would protect us when we were doing healing prayer.

God's Word stood. Neither Debbie nor I were affected by touching Eddy that day.

With my hand lightly on his right shoulder I sensed the Lord directing me how to pray. I began by taking authority over the infection.

I said, "In the name of Jesus, I bind that spirit of poison ivy and I order it to leave. You have no authority over Eddy's body. Your assignment is canceled. In the name of Jesus, I speak wholeness and health to Eddy and order any antibodies that fight this poison ivy, to multiply and heal Eddy's body from every trace of poison ivy.

"I plead the blood of the Lamb over Eddy's body, mind and spirit to shield him from the enemy."

I finished with, "Father, Jesus said we can ask You anything in His name. Now I'm asking that You bring complete healing to Eddy quickly, in the name of Jesus."

I finished with that and we left.

Less than two weeks later, Eddie called. He said, "Mama, you may not believe this, but the poison ivy is all gone, already. It's the worse case I've ever had but it cleared up sooner than it ever has. Thank you for coming and praying."

Debbie and I were thrilled to hear that Eddy's body was completely clear of poison ivy.

That was over 30 years ago. Eddy married a few years later, after completing college. He and his wife eventually had four sons. Eddy and his sons have enjoyed camping and exploring the woods in state parks around the country.

They are all avid hunters and fishermen, and tromp through the woods often. Once in a while Eddy has had small rashes. But he's never again had anything as severe as he had on that day that we prayed.

That was the first time I did a "hands on" healing prayer as the Bible instructs. Memories of it are still vivid.

I guess God needed to do something strong to show me that He was giving me a gift of healing and that has given an awesome sense of fulfillment to my life.

Chapter #14

A Surprise Song

"But no one says, 'Where is God my Maker, who gives songs in the night?'"   Job 35:10

This story is about healing of a man I never met. His wife was a dear friend of mine. A preacher's kid, Maggie was not into God's healing touch as I was, through the Charismatic movement.

She was my good friend and quietly listened to me when I excitedly told her of how God would bring healing to others as I prayed. That was why she chose to become God's vessel to help bring emotional healing to her dear husband. Here's how it happened.

"Let's set up these tables in a U-shape."

That came from Maggie, a strong leader, and considerate of others. She and I were preparing a church room for our first Writer's meeting of a new writers' group in Kansas City. As part of the leadership team we helped name it the Kansas City Christian Writers' Network.

Jeanette Gardner, had invited us both to help start it since we were writers for Youth For Christ devotional part of their magazine.

Maggie and I had met at a small gathering of the begining nucleus of these writers a few months earlier. We had instantly bonded.

She was a schoolteacher and had recently retired so she could focus on getting her poetry published.

Like Maggie, when my kids became grown and gone, I turned my focus to writing. But, as a divorcee I had to keep working to support myself.

Since all three of my children had taken jobs in other towns and moved their families far away, I fought loneliness. Being friends with Maggie helped. She became like an older sister, which I'd never had.

Even my parents and brothers lived in other towns far away.

When her husband Harold retired, Maggie's life suddenly changed dramatically. She stopped meeting me for coffee or lunch and became quiet at our meetings with writers.

Our telephone conversations came less often and her words were stilted. Her calls were brief. Her joyful nature was silenced. I was surprised that she sometimes even sounded grumpy.

Early in our relationship Maggie had spoken as if she was still very deeply in love with her husband Harold.

But when he retired her comments about him became negative.

One week-end that changed when we were driving to a big writers' conference in another town. She began opening up.

She suddenly said, "Sally, I'm so glad to be getting away from home for this conference. I've been feeling trapped. I love Harold to pieces but since he retired I don't feel I should leave during the day.

"I used to spontaneously jump in the car and go meet with my daughter, or you, or go shopping, or do whatever I wanted to.

"Now I don't feel free to leave Harold alone. He acts so depressed. The only reason I felt it was okay for me to come this week-end was that our daughter Diane was happy to have her dad stay at her house a few days."

Maggie's familiar friendly personality emerged during the three days at the conference. I was relieved to see her joyfulness return. We laughed together again.

Please Stop Praying

But on the way home she gradually withdrew and returned to her silence. As we approached the edge of our town she said, "Did I tell you Harold acts depressed?"

I nodded and said, "Yes, you have mentioned that. Do you want to tell me more?"

Shaking her head, she returned again to her silence.

A week later she called me. "Sally, I'd like to have you pray for me. I remember some of those stories you've told me about how God brings needed answers. I need that kind of prayer. When can we get together?"

We made an appointment for her to come to my home. Then I called my prayer partner, Sheryl, and arranged for her to join us. A prayer partner is important to me.

I had told Sheryl about Maggie's withdrawal since her husband's retirement. She was happy to come and made arrangment for her husband to care for their two young children that evening.

When Maggie arrived, I was not surprised to see her rigid and quiet. I suspected she might be frightened of being on the receiving end of healing prayer which I'd been telling her about. I could understand her hesitation. In fact, I was surprised that she had even asked for healing prayer.

When Sheryl came in I introduced her to Maggie. I was delighted that they seemed to bond easily.

Not only was Sheryl a small, pretty young mother, she had a loving attitude. She and I had prayed together with several people. So I let Sheryl explained our procedure.

Then I asked Maggie to tell us what she wanted us to pray about. She said Harold needed prayer but would never agree to come. She was mostly concerned about his quietness and depression. It made her feel trapped, like she had to stay home and take care of him.

She just wanted to stop feeling trapped.

Sheryl and I listened, letting her talk and answered her questions until we felt it was time for prayer.

But as we began to pray, Maggie seemed to become rigid, as if bracing herself protectively.

Tears often come when healing is received but, with Maggie, my box of tissues remained untouched as we finished praying that evening. Since she had ventured into the unknown by coming to me for prayer, I guess her adventurous spirit wanted to believe, but part of her couldn't because of her upbringing. She'd always gone to a basic church and hadn't experienced healing prayer.

When Sheryl and I prayed for someone we'd usually pray for nearly two hours. But that time we prayed for barely forty-five minutes.

I was curious about what God was going to do because I'd not heard His whisper as we began to close.

Nonetheless, we closed and I prayed for God's hand to be on Maggie and help her return to the friendly life-style she enjoyed. I trusted that eventually He would break through her barriers.

Then I said, "Lord, you know what Maggie needs today. You know what brought her here. You know she loves and trusts You. Please show her how to receive the healing You want to bring to her and Harold."

Those words were barely out of my mouth when suddenly Sheryl burst out singing "Zip-A-Dee-Do-Dah". She sang that entire chorus for a few minutes longer as we looked at her in surprise. She had a happy smile on her face as she sang. God had obviously whispered to her what was needed to bring the healing.

Suddenly tears began streaming down Maggie's cheeks. She broke out in a joyous grin. Apparently, that song had touched her heart. Her awareness that God really heard the prayers had brought her tears of relief. Sheryl finished singing. Then, her brows raised in curiosity, she said, "I hope that wasn't out of line. I felt the song just pop out and couldn't stop singing."

Maggie gently embraced her saying, "No, don't apologize. That's the song Harold whistles when he's in a good mood. Only Jesus could have known that."

The broad grin on her face spoke volumes.

Never again did Maggie doubt that God heard our prayers that day. Or that He wanted her to feel free again.

Within the next week Harold's depression lifted. As it did, Maggie began to enjoy her restored freedom of coming and going and visiting friends spontaneously. God seems to enjoy bringing the unexpected.

Chapter #15

Good Touch - Bad Touch

"Behold, children are a gift of the Lord; the fruit of the womb is a reward." Psalm 127:3

My daughter, Debbie, at age 17, fell in love with a handsome school mate. They went steady for nearly a year. As their high school graduation neared, Debbie was pregnant and her boyfriend was losing interest in her. Not interested in marriage or parenthood, he ran off and joined the Marines a week after they graduated.

I was grateful to have Debbie living with her teen brothers and I throughout her pregnancy. When her baby girl, Suzie, was born my heart filled with love for that tiny treasure.

After she was born I left Debbie at the hospital and headed for my office.

During that drive to work everything looked exceptionally beautiful. It was a delightful sunny October day. All the way to work I was praising God for his wonders in creating babies.

For the next three months Debbie, and little Suzie, lived at home with her brothers and I. She had a full time job in a fast food place. But she wanted to go to Junior College to begin her schooling to be a nurse. The best JuCo was across town so she decided it was time for her to move out on her own. Little Suzie was four months old.

Reluctantly, I helped her. It was a struggle saying good-by to them. I dreaded not getting to see them daily.

While holding down her job, Debbie began going to nursing school. I prayed for her success daily and for Jesus to protect both my daughter and her baby.

Debbie is very intelligent but, like her mother, made poor choices in romantic relationships. Sadly, her problems grew when she moved out on her own.

Having been raised with compassion for the needy, she took in a handsome young addict named Joe. He wasn't there long before he seduced her. But he had a violent personality with which we'd had no experience.

I'll never forget the Sunday I walked into our church and there sat my daughter with her face cut and bruised around her left eye from Joe having hit her. Even though I pleaded, she refused to ask him to move out.

With her lack of experience around thieves and addicts, she was a prime target for them. Eventually drug people sabotaged her car. Joe didn't have a car.

One day she passed out at work for unknown reasons. I had no knowledge of most of these things until years later. She had stopped confiding in me when Joe moved in. Of course, he even charmed her into giving him money since he wasn't working.

Through all of that, miraculously Debbie persisted in completing her schooling to become a nurse. For nearly two years I could only pray and honor her right to make her own choices.

But one day I had a call from her best friend. After talking with me politely a minute or so, she said, "Did you know Debbie has been evicted from her apartment and is living on the street with Joe and Suzie?"

I was shocked and even more worried about my daughter and her two-year-old child. My main thought was that I had to protect my little granddaughter.

My teenaged sons, Jim and Eddy, agreed to help me care for their niece if I got legal custody of little Suzie.

The next day, when I tried to call Debbie, her phone was disconnected, verifying what her friend had said. I called people to get prayer chains going.

One more day passed before she called me at work. I've always felt it had to have been because of the prayers.

When I recognized her voice I quickly said, "Debbie, you may be okay living on the street, but what about Suzie. She's just a toddler. Please bring her to me. Let me have legal custody. Your brothers and I have agreed to provide a good home for her until you get back on your feet." Finally she agreed and brought her little girl to me at my office.

It was a traumatic time for all of us. Getting the legalities taken care of went smoothly. Helping my two-year-old granddaughter get settled into our home was more difficult. But it didn't take long for my sons and I to develop a simple routine sharing her care.

I'd never had to find Day Care service since I'd been a stay-at-home Mom. But I found a good child care woman near my office. I began to feel my granddaughter was my own child.

But my sons were growing up and completing school. They would soon be gone, leaving me to be a single mother of a pre-schooler. Being the imperfect person that I am, I had my own struggles with that.

Soon Debbie put forth effort to get away from Joe. Earning her nursing degree brought her a good job easily. So she moved into another apartment. After a few months there, I agreed to let her have custody again since her daughter was nearing school age. I'd had her two years.

Then came the unexpected. A few months later Debbie announced that Joe had cleaned up his act, gotten a job and proposed.

But I knew he was deceptive. When he turned on his charming smile, Debbie believed whatever he said. I was never able to trust him.

Soon after they married, Debbie excitedly announced she was pregnant.

The following year when little Joe Jr. was born, his dad was obviously filled with pride. Barely two years later, she gave birth to another boy, Andy.

I knew in their marriage that Debbie and Joe had serious struggles but I kept my distance, praying that they'd work them out.

But on receiving her nursing degree she had been acting so much more mature. I trusted that to continue so

I stayed out of their struggles by focusing on my job and lay-ministry work.

I kept busy and grateful for my good job. And I also kept busy with a volunteer healing prayer ministry. Both helped me avoid interfering with their marriage.

God brought me hundreds of women asking for memory healing prayer. Many of them had been sexually abused as children.

Sexual abuse was foreign to me since I'd had a wholesome childhood. My own parents had been decent people. My dad was kind and treated me with respect. We had a wonderful relationship.

When I prayed for memory healing for other women, I became aware that I had been blessed with a healthy childhood and wholesome parents.

Doing memory healing prayer, I eventually became shockproof after hearing how fathers, cousins, grandfathers, uncles or step-dads sexually damaged little girls. As the girls matured most of them had kept her abuse a secret.

When they came to me for healing prayer, God showed me how to draw out the memories so He could heal them.

I began to see a pattern of posture and behavior of those who'd been hurt that way. That's why I became concerned about Suzie.

She was a beautiful little girl, nearing age ten when my suspicions were aroused. I noticed she acted self-conscious, keeping her eyes down. She covered herself in several layers of clothes and often kept her arms across her chest. Her hormones were becoming obvious in her chest.

I was very aware, over the years, that Joe had a strong sex drive.

By God's grace, when I noticed Suzie was covering herself, a local hospital advertised a solution which turned out to be a miracle. They were giving a presentation to help loved ones recognize and expose sexual abuse of children.

The play, called "The Land of Bubblionia", was created for children. It helped them to understand the difference between good and bad touching. The play provided guidance for a child to get help and told the importance of not keeping it secret.

Without telling Debbie of my suspicions, I asked if I could take Suzie to a drama presentation for children. She agreed, welcoming my interest as a grandmother.

Please Stop Praying

When I picked up Suzie that evening, I made a big deal of us having a fun night out together.

As we entered the hospital building she was very talkative, smiling a lot. The auditorium was small. As the presentation began I was pleased with the play they presented. It was done tactfully, on a child's level of communication.

When we left, Suzie was very quiet and withdrawn.

As I drove us home, after a brief silence, I said, "Well. What did you think of that play about good touching and bad touching? Did it make sense to you?"

More silence.

Suddenly almost crying, Suzie said, "Grams, who do I tell if someone is touching me the bad way?"

Her quick openness stunned me. Though that was the result I'd hoped for, I was amazed at how easily she spoke of this.

Pulling the car to the curb, I choked down my fears and growing anger at her stepdad. But I felt relieved that she was ready to talk so soon.

I slipped my arm around her and drew her close. Gently I explained, that she could tell her mother and I anything. I said that we were her "safe people" as they spoke of in the play. We both wanted to protect her.

Then she told me details of Joe's "bad touching" and how he continued even when she pleaded with him to not touch her. It had been going on for years, as I had suspected. I worked hard to hide the rage building up inside me toward her stepdad.

I was thankful I'd brought lots of tissues because we used them on both our tears that night.

I knew Debbie would be upset. So I told Suzie that I would tell her Mom. I promised her that her mom and I would work together to see that Suzie was safe from any more bad touching. I knew it must be done as quickly as possible.

Also I felt I explained that she shouldn't say anything to Joe. She needed to leave that to her mother. We had to be careful about how and when Debbie told Joe.

The sad part is that Debbie was pregnant at that time. When Joe left for work the next day, I met with her privately and told her about her husband's sexual abuse of her daughter.

At first she was angry at me and refused to believe it. But she soon admitted she'd also suspected it.

Then she told me she was confused about how to handle the matter.

She had a full time nursing job, three children at home and a six-month baby in her womb. Financially, she didn't feel she could move away from Joe until after her baby was born. One big factor was it was his job that provided health insurance which she needed to cover delivery of the baby.

I tried to talk her into leaving Joe immediately but she adamantly refused. Her attitude endangered Suzie. And it was very difficult for the child to understand. It was also hard for me to accept.

Sadly, at that time I was not able to offer to take my granddaughter into my home since I'd recently re-married.

Three months later, when little Abby was born, Suzie was excited about her new little sister. Debbie finally moved out. She went to great lengths to see that she and the children were safe and never in contact with Joe.

I went to her new place and helped care for them in the evenings for several weeks.

Shortly after they all were settled into their new routine, Debbie put Suzie in touch with her birth dad for the first time. That brought her first-born much joy and began a good relationship with her real father. They have maintained the long-distance communication. He has also made several trips to visit his only child.

When Suzie was 16 she was very involved in a good church. I was grateful that she was able to go on a teen missionary trip to a Native American Indian Reservation.

That week she led six adults to Christ. After all her childhood pains my lovely first granddaughter chose to serve and praise God.

Chapter 16

More Than a Face Lift

"For to one is given by the Spirit the word of wisdom; to another the word of knowledge by the same Spirit;" First Corinthians 12:8

"God speaks to us in many ways," I said to my adult Sunday school group. "His Word reaches each of us in a way we can understand. I hope you are reading His Word every day. He teaches us through His Word and through other people, in a still small voice. It's important that we take time to listen."

This was the first Sunday teaching my series about hearing God. As I spoke, a few people were arriving late.

One young man came in who had an unusual face. The "little green men" from outer space was the best way to describe him. Looking at him I almost forgot what I was saying.

His face looked smashed in. His chin was deeply receded, sticking out barely an inch from his neck. His hair-lip mouth was small and his nose barely protruded below two beady brown eyes that had thin lashes and small eyebrows.

He was barely five feet tall. With his narrow shoulders thrown back, his stubby arms swinging, he swaggered as if he dared anyone to say a word. His angry, cocky look was frightening yet he was dressed nicely and had beautiful thick brown wavy hair.

Since others were coming in right behind him, to hide my astonishment, I said, "We just started, folks. For those of you who are coming in, welcome."

Then I continued with my presentation.

After the class, he was among those who stayed to talk with me. He grinned, holding out his small, stubby-fingered hand for me to shake. With a slight lisp, he spoke confidently. "Hi I'm Michael. I liked your presentation."

His angry cocky look was gone and his confident attitude impressed me. I wanted to know him better and introduced him to Tim, my teaching partner.

I included Michael in my daily prayers for the people in the class. As I prayed one day, God whispered to me with startling clarity. "Tell Michael I will take a nip here and a tuck there and create a new face for him."

God had given me clear messages a few times before, so I recognized His voice and knew it was not my idea. But I definitely did not want to bring this message to a young man I had just met. How could I tell him this? How could I explain--even if I was sure it was from God? That thought frightened me. There was no way I would risk his anger.

That week I suppressed those words and didn't tell him after that Sunday's class. Of course, I was in turmoil. I knew God wanted me to pass those words on to Michael.

The next week as I prepared for class, God whispered to me again about Michael, "Tell Michael to read the joyful Psalms. There are woeful Psalms and joyful Psalms. Tell him he should be reading the joyful passages, as in Psalm chapters 81, 95 and 98."

I could do that. That Sunday when I went to class I was excited and eager to pass those new Words on to Michael. Obviously God wanted to communicate with him since He had given me two messages for him.

The Bible calls that "a word of knowledge", which is one of the gifts of the Holy Spirit. I was teaching about that.

Before class the next Sunday, I arranged with my partner Tim to be my male support person when I spoke with Michael. I felt joyful that he came to the class again. I asked him to stay afterward and talk.

I gave my teaching. Then, after the last person left, I was bursting with anticipation. Michael sat beside Tim looking expectant and curious

How to begin? Like a child, sometimes I tend to blurt out my thoughts when I get excited. But I knew I had to be calm and organized when giving God's Word.

With a wide grin I said, "Michael, do you remember the first Sunday when I announced that I pray for each member of the class?"

He nodded and began to grin with anticipation. "I also said that I'd be listening for any Word God might have for anyone."

Smiling and with a curious look, he nodded again. I was relieved to see he showed no anger.

Then I said, "Michael, God told me to tell you that there are joyful Psalms and woeful Psalms. He wants you to start reading the joyful Psalms. That would be Psalms 85, 95 and 98."

Michael's mouth fell open. Color drained from his face. He was speechless for a moment.

Then, with a wide grin, he said. "I can't believe this. That has to be from God. For months now I've been reading the woeful Psalms and crying out to God in anger."

Joy began flooding into all three of us. My heart was warmed with his words, yet part of me froze with hesitation. I knew I had to deliver the rest of the message. So I swallowed my fears and pride and continued.

"There's more," I said. "God also told me a couple of weeks ago to tell you He was going to 'take a nip here and a tuck there and give you a whole new face.'"

Again, a look of astonishment filled Michael's face.

"This is too much!" he exclaimed. His tiny mouth stretched into a broad smile.

He explained that a world famous cosmetic surgeon had recently examined him. Dr. Tessier from France specialized in reconstructive surgery from birth defects. That explained why he smiled so brightly. The doctor had laid out a plan to mold his face to look more normal. Michael was debating whether or not to go through with the surgery.

I had not known any of this. I was amazed as I saw Michael's defensiveness drop. He became animated as he shared with us, unloading his fears and frustrations about looking different from other people.

Listening to him tell about his struggles was so important that Tim and I forgot the time. The three of us were still talking an hour later. We had missed church service.

Then Tim invited Michael to join us for lunch with other singles from church.

That day was the beginning of a good friendship. Several of us got to know Michael. His arrogant anger was replaced with joy and joking. He had a delightful sense of humor.

A few months later Dr. Tessier was back in town. Michael eagerly anticipated his facial re-construction.

Our prayer team prayed for success for the surgery. Several of our singles decided to be there for him at the hospital, to bring him encouragement and comfort. I had to admit the new chin made him look better. It brought him a change of attitude. He was more relaxed and self-confident.

Over the next ten years, Michael had two more facial surgeries. Several of us, who were his friends, were always there for him. It became difficult for me to see him struggling with the pain from surgery. After the last one I suggested he looked good enough. He had a more normal chin and apparent cheekbones.

That face, topped with his beautiful head of hair, made him look more normal, though he would always look different. His body was short, with stubby hands and arms. But he was intelligent and enjoyed his work as a schoolteacher. He continued to have a good humor.

Without realizing it, I received healing of my attitude toward people who look different. God helped me become more accepting of them.

I learned that angry people are often afraid and only want someone to love them. I also learned that people who don't look as perfect as I think they should, are sometimes more lovable and interesting than those with the "normal" appearance.

That old cliche "Don't judge a book by its cover" may be worn out but it's still good advice. Michael may not have looked like most people, but he was a delightful friend. He really enjoyed being a school teacher.

Eventually I remarried and moved away to another church, losing track of Michael and other friends. But I'll always be thankful for his friendship.

Chapter #17

A Fallen Tree Brings Healing

"Honor your father and mother…"
Ephesians 6:1 and Exodus 20:12

My Mama didn't love me. At least that's what I thought until I was 54 and a tree fell on our old home in Oklahoma City. What happened after that brought me unforgettable good experiences. It had to be one of God's biggest lessons for me. I've often suspected He blew that tree over to bring healing to our relationship. Here's how it happened.

"Sally, sit still!" Mama's voice was harsh as she jerked my hair while braiding it. At age six, I choked back my sobbing so I'd be still and she wouldn't scold me more. She seemed to actually enjoy yanking my hair. My earlier plea that day, for no braids, had been ignored. Every time she braided my hair it was the same painful experience.

I was a quiet little kid. I never got spankings. But scolding and criticism seemed to be all that Mama ever said to me.

"Sit up straight!" "Don't chew your nails!" "Can't you do anything right?"

Compliments never came from her. It was no wonder I lacked self-confidence.

On the school playground, I was that timid little girl who stood at a distance chewing her fingernails.

Mama always seemed to be scolding my younger brother, Johnny. But our big brother, Dick, seemed to do no wrong. I don't know why.

By the time I was a teen, I hated Mama and fought my guilt feelings about it.

Balancing out her criticisms, Daddy was a gentle and honest man who always treated me with respect. He talked with me as if I was an equal—an adult. We had many meaningful conversations. He provided a modest income as a bookkeeper. But his joy came from being a Boy Scout leader, building small things in his basement workshop, and teaching my brothers how to play baseball.

In my late teens, I fell in love with an affectionate young man. Receiving wholesome affection made a drastic difference in my self-esteem.

After we married, I soon got pregnant. That's when I began reading books on touching and affection.

Please Stop Praying

My husband's first job after completing schooling was in a small town in Kansas. I was pregnant with my second child when we moved. Eventually we had three children and made annual trips back to our hometown, Oklahoma City.

That's when I began to hug my parents "Hello" and "Goodbye". I noticed they were each receptive to my hugs, though awkward. They even began to act like they liked being hugged.

My husband's parents were always sweetly affectionate. I learned much from them.

Having children helped me make a drastic change in my quiet nature. I gave them plenty of hugs and told them they were loved. I had grown up with neither of those. I quickly realized that it's vital to convey affection to a child.

Sadly, as my children were reaching their teens, their dad and I divorced.

After that, I often called my Daddy for advice. I never sought Mama's advice but she often gave it to me anyway. Mostly she tried to convince me that moving back to Oklahoma City would be good.

I was not going to do that. After living several years in Kansas City, I was settled in and happy there.

Over time Mama mellowed out, accepted it, and began saying more good things. That was a pleasant change.

Then Daddy died, and my world caved in. He had been the source of the most real love I'd ever felt. Then he was gone.

But life goes on. My children grew and my nest emptied. Feelings of loneliness and low self-esteem since childhood drove me to begin working with a psycho-therapist. Then I became involved with the recovery group called Adult Children of Alcoholics.

I'm suspecting my maternal grandfather had an alcohol problem, which I inherited.

I was amazed to hear other women reveal their hatred of their Mothers. And they spoke of cruelties in their childhood similar to mine. Many had been hurt much worse, physically, in childhood than I had.

Mama had never hit me. But her sharp tongue had pierced my self-worth again and again.

Those support group experiences healed my hatred of Mama. Emotionally, my understanding came eventually. It was as if I had slipped into the light after living in darkness all my life. I had thought I was the only person in the world who had been treated cruelly. I was humbled to hear of other women being treated much worse.

My relationship with Jesus grew deeper as I worked the 12-step program. He became my best friend. I knew He had led me into this recovery. After five years in that 12-step program, and nearly as long with a

therapist, I overcame my anger and resentment toward Mama. My trips to visit her in Oklahoma City became more pleasant.

Then came the unexpected. Mama had continued to live alone in our old homestead after Daddy died. Ten years later God used that to bring me an important lesson.

There was a major storm in our old neighborhood. A huge tree in Mama's backyard was uprooted and it fell on the house, destroying half the roof. The house insurance had expired because Mama had overlooked making the payment.

My brothers both still lived in Oklahoma City and decided they would have to repair the house in their spare time. Both in their fifties they had jobs, families and limited energy after working all day. That meant it would take a long time.

My older brother, Dick, and his wife moved Mama into a rental house of their's since it had just become vacant. Their younger son, Bryan, 19, had recently moved in there.

Mama was used to quiet in her home. She did not like having Bryan's gabby teen friends coming in and out at all hours. Nor did she approve of the blaring boom box.

A month after the tree fell, I made a trip to Oklahoma City to survey the damage and see how Mama was doing.

The damaged house was worse than I'd imagined. Memories flooded back of sweet times in our beautiful backyard. I left hurriedly with tears filling my eyes. I remembered times of sitting in the back yard, under that fallen tree, talking with Daddy for hours.

When I went to see Mama at the rental house, she was unusually quiet, and seemed very stressed. She had never liked change, having lived in the same old home over 40 years.

The next day on my way out of town, I stopped there to say goodbye. We talked about a half hour, then I headed for the door. I hugged her goodbye and turned to leave. She stepped into another room, returning quickly with her purse and a suitcase, which I didn't see. She followed me to the car.

Stepping around my car to get into it, I suddenly noticed the suitcase. Puzzled, I turned and asked, "Mama, what are you doing?"

"I'm going home with you until they fix my roof. I can't keep living with a teenager and all that noise."

Though I didn't like that, I knew better than to argue with her. I kept my mouth shut and let it happen. Acceptance was the answer, thanks to the healing of my attitude in recovery.

Once Mama made a decision, she had the stubbornness of a mule.

I had written her about my new two-bedroom apartment in a pleasant neighborhood.

It was as if God had said, "OK, Sally, you've done all the mental work to forgive your mother, now let's put it into practice."

After she lived with me a week, I moved my computer from the room I'd used as my office. I made a place for it in my bedroom, bought her a twin bed, and turned my writing office into Mama's bedroom.

That was when my 83-year-old Mama and I became roommates. We had verbal head-banging sessions but, surprisingly, life was fairly pleasant. I started giving her a routine hug at bedtime. She liked that.

My grown children came to visit often. Two of them and their families lived in Kansas City, as I did. They had grown up seeing my Mama as a loving old grandmother. I had to admit that she had mellowed into a more pleasant person since my childhood.

Soon after she moved in, I was aware that she had was no longer as critical. And she didn't act afraid to be touched or lovingly patted on the back. She acted pleased when one of my grandchildren wanted to sit in her lap. It seemed as if God had been working on Mama while He worked on me.

During her three years with me, we had some good family times at my daughter's home, especially over the holidays. I also have to admit that Mama's help with the basic expenses reduced some of my financial stress.

But some days I'd come home from work to find coiling clouds of smoke poured out my apartment door.

Filling my nostrils with the stink of burning food, I shouted, "What's burning?" Smiling comically Mama

Please Stop Praying

ducked her head with a mocked sorry look. Then she said "I forgot that I'd left the green beans cooking when I was watching my soap operas."

She really stretched my patience. I learned a lot about old-age forgetfulness during those days. Her total dependence on me was sometimes overwhelming.

When she had a health issue, as usual, she ignored it and said nothing until it was serious. When I discovered shingles on her back, I fussed at her for not telling me sooner. She argued with me that she didn't need a doctor. I finally won and took her to my doctor.

Over time, being her sole caregiver, I came to feel love and affection for Mama.

After 3 years of living together, we had routinely hugged goodnight. One evening she stepped back and looked at me and kissed my cheek. That was a first.

She said, "Sally, I'm so glad that tree fell on my house. Otherwise I wouldn't have gotten to know you as an adult."

Then she said, "I love you, Sally," for the first time in my life. What a treasured moment! She hadn't done that before and never did it again. That and our once-in-a-lifetime kiss, made me thankful that I had been patient with her.

A few weeks later my brothers had Mom's house repaired and livable. It had taken them three years. They didn't hurry. Maybe they were relieved to not have to take care of Mama personally while she was with me. She moved back to Oklahoma City and lived there alone another ten years.

When she died, at age 94, I felt a great love for her and healthy grief. I was relieved that I no longer felt guilty for hating her so many years.

My healing did not happen quickly or easily. It happened with the help and counsel of many people, and lots of prayers.

I've learned that forgiveness is imperative for good health. God brought me the lesson I needed. I'm grateful He made that tree fall to bring our healing.

Chapter #18

Resting In the Spirit

"For we which have believed do enter into rest, as he said." Hebrews 4:3

"How many of you have rested in the Spirit? Sometimes it's called "Slain in the Spirit", but I prefer the softer version of "resting"".

The question had come from British Reverend John Bedford. He was the teacher at a healing seminar I was attending in Chicago. I had come to this training with the Healing Team from my church in Kansas City, Missouri.

As Rev. Bedford asked his questions, a few hands were raised in response. Mine wasn't one. Though I did healing prayer for others at church I knew very little about this subject.

The Rev. had traveled all the way from England to bring this teaching to us. I was in his class seeking to learn more. Though I'd not heard much teaching about it

I had seen people at my church fall into the healing trance. I had finally decided I needed to know more about "resting in the Spirit".

Back home, on Sunday evenings our prayer team, had healing services. I was part of that team. I'm still awed when I see how God heals so differently every time.

At my church at that time, on those evenings we had three lines of people waiting for our three prayer teams. I had at least two assistants to catch those who "rested in the Spirit". I never knew what the person on the floor was experiencing. Frankly, I'd been a little afraid to ask for that myself.

That's why I was in Rev. Bedford's class. I was ready to ask the Lord to show me how to "rest in the Spirit".

This minister's sincerity and gentle, unassuming manner enchanted me. He reminded me of my kind daddy who was no longer living. Having studied Bedford's background I was interested in learning from him.

Though I questioned the value of this topic, I respected his faith and experience. I hoped that his teachings would help me decide that it might be Spiritualy valid. But part of me wondered what the point was. Did it bring healing? Part of me wanted to believe that it did.

It was similar to when I questioned if I could speak in tongues. When I relaxed and asked God about that "Spiritual Gift" He had done something unexpected to bring me the needed teaching and the gift of tongues.

That day, in Chicago, sitting in Bedford's class, I was seeking to have that experience since it was acceptable in my Charismatic church.

Bedford explained that this is sometimes the only way the Lord can get through to us as intimately as we need. The Holy Spirit knocks us down and we go into a trance-like state so we can hear Him better.

Sometimes people are so thick-headed, giving up part of our self-control is a big step. Though we may be afraid, sometimes we hide it with an attitude of rebellion. Deep inside I knew that was my problem.

He said, "When a person goes down, we who are ministering are not to touch them. That allows the Holy Spirit better clearance to lay them down."

Please Stop Praying

But he suggested, when someone is down, one person who is praying should get down on the floor beside them. We should quote Scripture or make soothing comments to let them know they're safe.

As Bedford concluded his teaching, he made the offer, "If anyone wants me to pray for them, or ask a question, please line up over there. He pointed to a spot near the door.

Curious, and wanting this experience, I stood in line and waited my turn. Most of those ahead of me just asked questions and left after a brief chat. I felt myself growing more eager.

When I stepped in front of Rev. Bedford, about a half dozen people were standing around the room chatting. Looking into his kind face, I said "I just wanted you to pray for me to rest in the Spirit here."

"Why do you want to do this?" He asked with a loving smile.

That threw me off guard. I hadn't expected that question. But, with a sheepish grin, I admitted, "I just want to know God can knock me down."

His smile dropped. He said, "Well, I must tell you, the Lord will not honor that reason."

I cried "Oh, No! I want it. I…"

Instantly, I felt as if a huge hand had been cupped along my back and picked me up. I was gently lowered to the floor. It took only a second.

What was amazing was that I'd been standing with my back about a foot from an inside corner between two doors. Yet I didn't fall against it. I could have hit my head on a sharp corner. But I was lifted up and laid down and went into a trance. There was no human behind me.

My eyes were closed and I sensed a rich male voice speaking deep inside my head. I heard things that made me laugh and cry at the same time.

As he had instructed us, I heard Bedford beside me down on the floor. He said, "Just take in the love of Jesus, my dear. Breathe in His strength and healing."

I kept chuckling and felt so loved. I had a sense of being scolded but with humor and love. It seemed to last 20 or 30 minutes but when I finally awoke, and sat up, it had only been about five minutes.

I felt warmly nurtured, as if I'd been touched by the Master as never before. But I had received no physical touch.

Struggling to my feet, a man nearby helped me up. Though young, in my 40s, and strong, I felt weak and wobbly.

Please Stop Praying

Bedford stood in front of me smiling. He said, "I'd encourage you to go some place quiet and alone to process what has just happened here. When you know what it was that you were laughing about, I'd like to hear. I've never known that to happen before."

Later, in the church yard, I sat alone under a tree, shaded from the warm summer sun. I knew I needed to absorb that unusual experience. What kind of healing had come that way?

Sitting there I asked the Lord to explain what had just happened. A chuckle came from me as if it was a leftover.

I remembered, when I answered Bedford's question of why I wanted to "rest in the Spirit", how disappointed I was at his response.

That was when the Lord literally laid me down saying, "The true child inside you began to plead for Me to bring you down. You silly goose. That's why you're here."

That was why I had laid there laughing and crying. I was filled with gratitude of the awesome love that God showed me that day.

Then the Lord went on to say, "Don't be so arrogant. You have much to learn. Sally, you have a problem of rebelliousness. I want you to work on that. You may be 48 years old but you need to remember that, to Me, you're just a child.

"I'm grateful you trust Me to do the healing that you call on Me to do. You're faith will carry you far. But don't be so obstinate. Call on Me and I will answer you. Sometimes I will say 'No' and sometimes I will say 'Wait'. And you know when I say 'Yes'."

At church that evening when I told John Bedford why I laughed, he chuckled and said, "That makes sense. I understand. The Lord truly loves you and you obviously love Him and desire to serve."

I left Chicago with a very different attitude. I felt as if I'd been put in my place. But it took more than that for me to let go of a particular area of my life where I was rebellious. That's in another chapter.

I contend that each person has the right to be as involved with the Lord as much as they wish. There's no need to be fake or do what isn't comfortable. Just having a relationship with Jesus and knowing His voice is what's important.

Chapter #19

Blind More Ways Than One

"Thou blind Pharisee, cleanse first that which is within the cup and platter, that the outside of them may be clean also." Matt 23:26

"How long have you been blind, Virginia?" I asked my new friend. We were having coffee at a local café. She'd been telling me about her job as a schoolteacher and her struggles adjusting to deterioration of her vision.

"It's been about two years now," she said, sipping from her cup. "Some day I'll have you come and pray for that.

"But today I need prayers for my ongoing struggle with my folks. I've dealt with their arguing with me all my life. That's why I moved out on my own right after high school. My life seems to be going just fine until Mom calls. We always end up fighting. I'm tired of it."

We made a date for me to come to her home to pray. As we left the café she picked up her white and red walking stick and adeptly found her way to the door and to my car.

A week later, after arranging for intercessory to be praying, my prayer partner, Marcia and I went to

Virginia's house. As we began to pray, Virginia folded her arms across her chest as if blocking the door to her heart to keep healing from coming in. She had asked for healing. But her body position said, "No Way!"

As we prayed I told what I envisioned. Jesus was beside Virginia explaining to her what her mother was trying to say. But Virginia refused to accept responsibility for any of their disagreements.

As I prayed for her I felt Jesus was saying that the words all seemed to be thrown against a brick wall.

Marcia and I both sensed the need to cut it short. We ended the prayer time and left. As she drove we spoke of our frustrations. Before we parted we prayed for healing between Virginia and her parents. Later I passed that need on to other intercessors.

A few months later, Virginia asked us to come and pray for her blindness. She had just seen another doctor and they could not find the reason for her blindness.

Marcia and I discussed whether or not we should try again. We both hoped for Virginia to have a different attitude so we went.

Once again we were disappointed. Virginia sat rigid with her arms across her chest again. It was a duplicate of our previous prayer time, as if everything was blocked.

Please Stop Praying

Marcia and I decided God would have to make an obvious change in Virginia's attitude before we would make the trip over to pray for her anymore.

Instead we agreed to do daily intercessory prayer. The next day I spoke aloud to the Lord about my frustrations with Virginia. When I'd encountered that blockage when praying for other people, God seemed to relax the arms of the person. Some way God enabled others to receive healing. But not Virginia.

As I prayed for Virginia, God clearly gave me a word of knowledge. "She doesn't really want to see inside or out."

For some reason, known only to God, she felt safer keeping her blindness.

How do we see? With the eyes, of course. But we also see with the heart. Pondering that fact helped me stop feeling like a failure.

Shortly after that prayer time, God brought Tom into Virginia's life. They met at church. He was a Christian, and a quiet, gentle man who adored Virginia. He was comfortable with her blindness.

About a year after their friendship began, they were married. Being married seemed to bring Virginia some contentment. When I'd see her at church she was mellowing out and developing a sense of humor.

Since there had been no clear diagnosis of why Virginia was going blind, she continued to seek new doctors. Some of them determined it was "hysterical blindness", meaning it came from deep emotional problems.

One day she called and said, "Sally, I need prayers again. It's about my mom. Tom has been acting as a bridge between my folks and me. They've even been coming here to visit and it's been amazingly pleasant. With him I'm able to handle their criticisms.

"But a couple of months ago we went to my folks' for supper. At their house everything happened just like it used to. Mom and I butted heads again and yelled like we've done for years. I hated it. Tom and I left and I've not talked with them since. Something has to give. Can you come and pray for me again, please?"

My heart went out to her. Her tone seemed more loving and less rigid. Then she surprised me by saying, "I know Jesus can mend this broken relationship."

I'd never heard her speak with such a positive attitude. I agreed to come.

Marcia and I were hopeful as we drove to her home. As we began to pray, I was delighted to see Virginia's hands resting in her lap in a receptive attitude.

Praying, we took her back to a time in her teen years when she and her mother were in one of their heavy disagreements. When Jesus came into the vision, He stood between them. I could tell Virginia was mentally back in that time which meant she was healing.

Taking her hand, Jesus said, "Honor your mother. She's trying to protect you from making serious mistakes that she made at your age."

The stubbornness on the Virginia's face was quickly replaced with surprised understanding.

Then we envisioned Jesus taking her mother's hand and saying "You have a brilliant daughter who is as stubborn and independent as you have always been.

"Today you have the maturity to see she loves you because she keeps trying to re-build your relationship. Show her the wisdom of your years and be grateful.

We envisioned her mother's eyes opening wide, as if they had suddenly been filled with undeniable truth and she understood.

That evening a miraculous healing happened with Virginia's attitude. As we finished, it was obvious she was deeply touched and received healing as never before. She kept reaching for tissues to wipe away her tears. For the first time, our prayers with her had not been in vain.

The miracle became complete the following week. Virginia called.

Bubbling with joy she said, "You won't believe what's happened. My mother called yesterday and we talked easily for the first time ever!

"She actually apologized! I don't understand it, but she acted as if she had been with us when Jesus brought that healing last week. She talked about the problem exactly as Jesus had spoken of it.

"We met for coffee within an hour and hugged. I don't remember ever hugging my mother as an adult." Marcia and I felt relieved that healing had happened.

Since then I've lost touch with Virginia and have wondered if her physical eyes were ever healed. At least I take comfort in knowing the emotional healing was received between she and her mother that day. That's God's perfect timing.

Chapter #20

Miracles of Brain Surgery

"And we know that God causes all things work together for good to those who love God, to those who are called according to His purpose." Romans 8:28

My world fell apart when I was thirty-six. My 17-year marriage ended in divorce and I turned to alcohol.

That addiction ruled me for twelve years, distorting my judgment.

Like the Biblical "woman at the well", I tried marriage four more times. Each ended in divorce.

Entering A.A. in 1983, I not only became sober, I became healthier emotionally. God brought me an excellent professional psycho-therapist who was a friend from church.

On my 64th birthday I settled into retirement. But, with no husband, I couldn't shake my desire for male attention.

Please Stop Praying

A year later, December, 1999, I was confused and prayed, "Lord, please take away my obsession for male attention."

January 2000, working at my computer, suddenly I saw the typed words floating on the monitor screen. A stabbing pain pierced my left temple.

Headaches are rare for me, so I was frightened and confused. I hurried to the bathroom for aspirin. Instead, I stripped and climbed into the shower. Under running water, I remembered I'd already showered an hour earlier.

Confused, I climbed out, dried, dressed, and went to my phone. I knew talking with a friend would help me figure out what was happening.

Looking through my personal phone book, I couldn't recognize any name. More confused, I collapsed into my recliner.

Thirty minutes later, my thinking seemed to clear. Guessing it might be an eye problem, I decided to call my optometrist.

I was surprised that I found her number in my phone book immediately with no problem. I was even more surprised that she had an appointment opening the next morning. She had never had an opening sooner than three weeks. I took that one.

The next morning, she examined my eyes while listening to my story of head pain and confusion the day before.

Finally she said, "Your eyes are fine, Sally. But from what you've said, I'm concerned that you may have had a stroke or something worse. You need to go to the hospital directly from here."

I did.

Doctors ordered many tests. Their diagnosis was that I had an egg-sized brain tumor behind my left ear. It needed to be removed.

My three grown children live in other towns with their jobs and families. But two of them lived close enough to come and escort me to the hospital for surgery.

It took six hours to remove the meningioma.

Joyce and Harold, friends from church, cared for me in their home for the week after surgery.

My son, Scott, had taken my cat, Woody, to care for him until I was back home.

The week after surgery, I was missing Woody and my familiar surroundings. I called my surgeon and asked if I could go home though I lived alone.

After asking me several questions, he gave me permission and reminded me of his list of post-surgery limitations. That was handed to me before I left the hospital a week earlier.

Joyce and Tom, the couple who were caring for me, tried to get me to stay another week. But I was missing my familiar surroundings and was feeling stronger. And I am a stubbornly independent person.

Reluctantly, the next day Joyce drove me to my apartment.

Living alone was not as easy as I'd expected. Surgery had made me cross-eyed so I had to wear an eye patch. That was the uncomfortable and I didn't like having the eye covered, but it helped.

I was weak, wearied easily, and my thinking was muddled. Worst of all, I was unable to drive. And stairs had to be avoided. I was no longer full of energy as usual. As the doctor had advised, I needed lots of rest. He didn't add that resting would mean I'd need lots of help.

The good news is that during my recovery time I experienced many miracles. They began that day the words began floating on my computer screen and pain hit me. God had given me that speedy appointment with my eye doctor after just 30 minutes of symptoms.

Miracles also began happening the day after I returned home. That first morning I realized I couldn't do laundry. The apartment laundromat was in the basement.

I prayed aloud. "Lord, how am I going to do laundry? I can't do stairs or carry that heavy load." Leaving it in God's hands I turned on TV.

A few minutes later, I had a call from Margaret, a retired neighbor and friend. "Sally," she said, "I'm getting ready to do my laundry and realized you might need help with that. Do you want me to do yours?

Of course I said "Yes". So for five weeks my laundry was picked up, washed and returned to me. It was even neatly folded.

Later that afternoon, I said, "Lord, I need to get groceries but I can't drive. What am I going to do?"

Within the hour Linda, from church, called and said, "Sally, you probably need groceries. Do you want me to come over tomorrow morning and take you to the store?"

Please Stop Praying

Of course I was delighted and we agreed on a time.

She transported me for groceries the next five weeks. She also worked with me to make a list of duties others could do, like cleaning, giving me rides, etc.

When my son brought Woody back, my furry roommate sensed my weakness. Jumping into my lap, he rubbed his cheek on mine which was his special greeting.

Usually Woody spent the day in the closet and explored outside all night. But for five weeks he stayed near me. Rather than run and hide when someone knocked at the door, he walked beside me. When I opened it, he would step in front of me as if to protect me.

Over the next few weeks, as I became stronger, Woody returned to his old routine; sleeping days, playing outside at night. Had God told him I was well?

Every day for six weeks, when I needed anything, I told God, and always, within an hour, someone would call and offer help for that very thing. All the calls were perfectly timed.

One friend called and asked if I needed a ride to the doctor's office, another offered to take me to church, another to support groups. Another called and asked if she could clean my bathroom. Another called asking to come and clean my kitchen. One had just bought a new vacuum and wanted to come over and vacuum my home.

Sometimes those coming to help brought me food. Five weeks of recovery showed daily miracles.

Eventually my vision cleared and I became stronger. But I was frustrated that low energy kept me from keeping my kitchen clean.

One day, dirty dishes filled the sink. Both stove and floor were a mess.

Then Marv called. He's the comical husband of Leona. They're a delightful retired couple from church who had helped me often.

"Hi Sally," Marv said cheerfully. "Leona and I wondered if you needed help cleaning your kitchen today."

My pride made me say, "No. I've got it covered. But thanks for calling."

I hung up and was immediately convicted. I needed help but was too proud to admit it. I felt God scolding me for lying and reminding me that I'd asked His help.

Please Stop Praying

So I called them back.

Leona answered. I said, "I lied just now. My kitchen's a mess. I'd really appreciate y'all coming and cleaning it."

Always understanding, with a joyful voice, she said "We'll be right there."

Just 20 minutes later, they pulled up in front of my apartment.

Slim and beautiful, Leona, slipped out of the driver's seat and came in smiling. She said "Hi" patting my shoulder, and headed straight for the kitchen.

Behind her, Marv moved more slowly, as usual. He has macular degeneration, making him partially blind. He made his way in by himself, with his constant broad grin.

I sat in my recliner facing the patio door soaking in the sunshine.

As he came in, smiling, I said, "Hi Marv."
He came over and put his big hands on my shoulders.

Neither of us was able to focus or see the other clearly. But he aimed his face toward mine and said,

"Sally, we're so glad you called back. We want you to know you nearly robbed us of the blessing of helping you."

He grinned and headed for the kitchen.

I chuckled thanking him.

Marv's sweet attitude, delivering that fact, showed me another blessing. He reminded me that allowing others to help us brings blessings to those who give.

I experienced so many miracles during my recovery. Over six weeks I'd had dozens of these awesome coincidences. How could I not believe God is still in the miracle business?

When my story started I said I'd never marry again. God renounced that vow.

Three years later our heavenly Father brought me my only husband this century. As of today, we've been married eight and one-half unbelievable years.

That will be another story.

Dear Reader:

To God be the Glory. I pray that everyone reading this will have a new or renewed relationship with Jesus Christ. If you want to connect with me I am on Facebook.

Or you can check my blog at

www.sallysdoor.vpweb.com

Made in the USA
Monee, IL
25 April 2025